SERVING WITH
HONOR

Performing Your Ministry with Integrity on
Your Way to Fulfilling God's Destiny for Your Life

ANDREW G. ROBBINS

authorHOUSE®

AuthorHouse™
1663 Liberty Drive
Bloomington, IN 47403
www.authorhouse.com
Phone: 833-262-8899

Published by AuthorHouse 01/19/2022

ISBN: 978-1-5462-0665-1 (sc)
ISBN: 978-1-5462-0664-4 (e)

Print information available on the last page.

1

Introduction and Purpose

Constancy. Steadfastness. Stability. Perseverance. Loyalty. Dependability. Self-denial. Vision.

These words represent some of the most fundamental principles of Scripture and the teachings of our Lord Jesus. Yet these are concepts largely lost to contemporary Christianity. As a result, countless Christians go around the same mountains over and over and fail to fulfill God's ultimate destiny for their lives because they don't understand what it takes to fulfill that destiny.

Let me say right from the start that God has a call on your life, and that call is not dependent on your background, your experience, or your level of intelligence. God has chosen you. Before the creation of the world He had in mind the role you would play in His Kingdom. Don't ever forget that. You are chosen!

> *⁴For He chose us in Him before the creation of the world to be holy and blameless in His sight. In love ⁵He predestined us for adoption to sonship through Jesus Christ, in accordance with the pleasure of His will.*
> **-Ephesians 1:4-5** (NIV)

> *¹As a prisoner for the Lord, then, I urge you to live a life worthy of the calling you have received...⁷But to each one of us grace has been given as Christ apportioned it. ⁸This is why it says, "When He ascended on high, He took many captives and gave gifts to His people." ¹⁶From Him the whole body, joined and held together by every supporting ligament, grows and builds itself up in love, as each part does its work.*
> **-Ephesians 4:1,7,8,16** (NIV)

It is vital for you to remember that you were called and given a role in the Body of Christ. You were saved to serve! Equally important to remember is your role, whether big or small, will always be connected in some way to the local church, directly or indirectly. The passage just quoted from Ephesians 4 says the whole body is joined and held together by every supporting ligament, meaning you and me. The Apostle Paul, who penned those words by revelation of the Holy Spirit, was talking about the church. Ministry flows from the church.

Many of God's people know they have a call on their lives. I'm probably not telling you anything you don't already know on this point. Yet too many Christians have only a vague sense of what their calling is, and/or are frustrated in arriving there or even getting started on that process because they so often sabotage their own progress. Many live out their lives in a nebulous state of disappointment and frustration because the dreams and callings they sense in their hearts never came to pass.

This unfortunate situation has a ripple effect on whole churches, because when people do not have an understanding of what they have been called to do or what the path leading to the fulfillment of that call requires of them, it leaves people without a sense of direction. When this happens, God's people too easily hop around from one church to another trying to find themselves and striving endlessly to arrive at their personal Promised Land.

The Church of Jesus Christ, therefore, has been weakened by shallow commitments mingled with self-serving motives. Many churches struggle to fill important ministry positions, and God's people suffer the consequences of overworked pastors and less-than-stellar results of ministry work.

For pastors and leaders, one of the ongoing frustrations in churches is the constant flow of people going in and out of important ministry positions. It seems like many people are by nature transient in their church lives for a variety of reasons. One reason for this, as already stated, is people so often church-hop trying to find themselves or trying to find a "perfect" church, which doesn't exist, of course. But another common reason for this tendency is due to the ignorance among God's people in the West about the spiritual importance of the words with which I opened this book: constancy, steadfastness, stability, perseverance, loyalty, dependability, and self-denial in the midst of uncomfortable circumstances.

People also tend to be transient because we as a culture have become fair weather friends due to being raised in homes where fathers and sometimes even mothers are missing in action. Our dysfunctional upbringings have taught us to look out for "number one" regardless of who it might hurt and to move on when it suits us. There is a tremendous amount of ignorance in the body of Christ on the subject of stability and commitment. And any time there is ignorance there is also the possibility of destruction. ***"My people are destroyed for lack of knowledge,"*** says Hosea 4:6.

Therefore, when someone who is manning an important ministry position decides to move on but leaves a hole in the church in doing so, it harms the body and leaves the pastor or other leaders scrambling to try to fill the gaps, often in ways that are starkly less effective than the previous leader. When this happens and a pastor's trusted leader or ministry worker announces their departure, most pastors suck in their guts and say through gritted teeth and forced smiles, "Well, we'll miss you; be blessed." This is how pastors are *supposed* to respond, isn't it? It is apparently not considered gracious for pastors to tell people the truth in those kinds of situations because of the appearance of being self-serving or insensitive. What many pastors don't have the opportunity to say in those situations are the things I will say here in an effort to apply some preventive medicine – hopefully in an understanding, sympathetic, and loving way – and help everyone who mans an important ministry position at your church to gain a Kingdom perspective on what you are doing, what it means to God and His Church, and why it's important to do things God's way and not our own way.

To this end, we will undergo a thorough review of Scripture to gain a Kingdom perspective on what God has to say about the following:

- How God wants His church well manned by reliable and stable people.
- How God feels about leaving unmanned holes in His churches.
- What His Word says about loyalty, and the consequences of disloyalty.
- Why an undesirable circumstance in which people sometimes find themselves is often the very place God wants them in order to chisel their character and prepare them for future promotion in His Kingdom.

I should pause to clarify that I am not addressing people here who have fluctuating work schedules and who therefore serve in their churches irregularly. I realize this is a significant challenge in today's world of business where workloads are often very heavy and schedules are hectic and difficult to plan around. If you are a person who understands the importance of service to your church and your community but whose work schedule is heavy and/or always changing, this book is not necessarily for you. This book is for the purpose of preventing and addressing something I call a "Nomad spirit."

The Nomads were people who wandered as a way of life and never settled anywhere for any length of time. There are a lot of people in the Church today with a Nomad spirit in regard to their church involvement, and it severely inhibits, if not kills, their progress in the ministry and in the Kingdom. They wander around and land in a church for a time thinking this might be "it." But then something happens they don't like, or the grass looks greener on the other side for whatever reason, and they move on. And the process goes on and on like this for years. Before long a person with a Nomad spirit has 5 to 10 churches under his belt in just a few years, never understanding why he can't find a place he can call home. He has become a wanderer, a spiritual vagabond with a sense of calling but nowhere to put it to good use.

The Nomad Spirit, however, doesn't just manifest in church hopping. The Nomad Spirit often makes people feel restless and discontent as a way of life. It makes people discontent in their marriages and careers. These people may do as much hopping around in their careers or in multiple marriages as they do churches. And the wake of damage it leaves behind bears a heavy toll on their lives. I believe one reason why the Holy Spirit inspired me to write this book, therefore, is to help spiritual vagabonds understand how they have hindered their own calling and what to do to turn it around.

This book was ultimately birthed as a result of one simple phrase God spoke to me on which I will elaborate in the next chapter. After He spoke, I sat down to write, because writing is how I process things. Before I knew it, I had ten pages of content on what I felt God was trying to accomplish in both me and others in the Body of Christ, and those ten pages eventually turned into the book you are now holding. It still amazes me how God can kill several birds with one stone, so to speak, and how one simple but profound statement from Him can generate pages and pages of content as we unravel all the truth found in that statement.

Let's now turn our attention to what God said to me, and why it's an eternally important perspective for you and your ministry position.

2

"What People Do to My Church, They Do to Me"

On the morning of Thursday, July 20th, 2017, at approximately 6:30 a.m., I distinctly heard the Lord speak to my spirit. Before I elaborate on what He said, let me first explain how God speaks and how I heard Him, since this is a foreign concept to much of today's Church.

I did not hear an audible voice, and God did not appear to me. The Holy Spirit spoke a phrase to my spirit, and I "heard" Him in my heart.

I believe God has spoken and perhaps still speaks to people audibly sometimes, however. He certainly did so with many people in the Bible. I also believe angels still appear to people on occasion and speak on behalf of God as they did in Bible times. God also speaks in dreams as He did with Joseph and many others in the Bible, which has happened to me numerous times. God also speaks through other people, He certainly speaks through His written Word, and He speaks in word pictures and in giving His people a sense of direction in their hearts. He also speaks through words and phrases spoken *inaudibly* to one's spirit.

More often than not God directs me through the Bible, but I have also had impressions and a sensing in my spirit about certain things, and less often I'll have dreams, as I said. It's only on the rare occasion where God will interrupt a train of thought and sort of suddenly arrest my attention by speaking a phrase to my spirit when I wasn't even thinking about what He was addressing.

This is what happened to me on that summer morning when I sensed God speaking. I had just risen from bed and was still bleary-eyed as I was preparing to embark upon my morning routine of hot tea and a banana before my time of prayer and Bible study. I was in the kitchen heating up some water, not thinking about anything in particular, when suddenly this phrase struck my mind:

"What people do to My church, they do to Me."

Huh? I had to stop and think about this for a moment. That thought had never crossed my mind, so I had to pause and ponder it. I had never really thought about this concept, at least not in those terms. I have on occasion taught and wrote about people esteeming the meeting of the local church, and those who lightly esteem the meeting of the church lightly esteem Jesus, because the Church is the Bride of Christ. The attitude a person has about the local church is the attitude they have about Jesus. I understood all this on a surface level, but this was the first time I ever thought about how it affected God.

When God spoke to me, He took the concept a lot further than I had ever considered it. Again, He said, **"What people DO to My church, they DO to ME."** Therefore, God does not just concern Himself with the *attitudes* we have about His church and our frequency of attendance. He also concerns Himself with our *actions* toward and in the church. His words that morning produced one of those "wow" moments of revelation for me which I will elaborate on here.

In order to validate it when someone says, "God spoke to me," I feel it's important to be able to cross reference whatever a person thinks God said against the Scriptures. After all, it's very easy to say God said something when in reality what a person thinks God said could violate one or many scriptural principles. This goes on all the time, by the way. People will often say God said this or that, when it is actually emotion speaking, or something else. I have on occasion been guilty of this. So, on the same morning I sensed God was speaking to me about His church, I immediately went to work in my mental files to see if I could cross reference what I thought He said against a scriptural story or principle. It only took me about five seconds to start remembering instances in the Bible where this phrase, "what people do to My church, they do to Me," played out.

Perhaps the best example is Saul of Tarsus before his conversion and name change to Paul. You might recall that Saul was a fierce persecutor of the first-century Christians. He ordered them dragged out of their homes and thrown into prison. Some were executed. Saul was later confronted with the glorious presence of the resurrected Jesus and heard these words from the Savior: "Saul! Saul! Why are you persecuting **ME**?" Then Saul replied, "Who are you, lord?" And the Son of God replied, "I am Jesus, the one you are persecuting." (See Acts 9.)

Saul had never laid eyes on Jesus. He certainly never had an opportunity to directly persecute the Lord when Jesus was on the earth in the flesh. Yet Saul's behavior toward the church was considered by Jesus as a direct attack against Him. Jesus took it personally!

Another instance in the New Testament where the actions someone took against the church was taken very personally by God is found in Acts chapter 5. This is the account of a married couple by the name of Ananias and Sapphira. This is a famous story you probably know well. This couple sold some property and gave a portion of the revenue to the church but told the church leaders they had given the entire amount, which was an obvious attempt to make the contribution look better and more spiritual than it actually was. The apostle Peter, sensing by the Holy Spirit what had been done, then confronted Ananias and exposed his actions. Peter ended his short and direct diatribe to Ananias by saying, "You have not lied to man, but to God." You know the outcome. God slew Ananias on the spot, and then later his wife when she came in and gave a false testimony of her own.

Now wait a minute! Ananias and Sapphira spoke to the *church leaders* when they lied. They weren't speaking directly to God... right?

We have to understand that the church leaders represented an extension of God's authority, and the Church itself is the Bride of Christ. Therefore, in God's mind, what Ananias and Sapphira did to the church and its leaders, they did to God.

Are there other examples of this same sort of thing happening elsewhere in Scripture? Yes!

Do you remember the story in Numbers 12 when Moses' siblings, Aaron and Miriam, rose up against him? They spoke out against Moses because he was doing things they didn't like. Now get this: **They believed they were justified** in their complaints against Moses because their issue was him having married a Cushite woman who was not part of the covenant of Israel. They got hopping mad because Moses had married a Gentile. In their minds their cause was merited, and they were perfectly justified to be

> **We have to understand that the church leaders represented an extension of God's authority, and the Church itself is the Bride of Christ. Therefore, in God's mind, what Ananias and Sapphira did to the church and its leaders, they did to God.**

angry with Moses and speak out against him. But notice God's response. He said, *"Why then were you not afraid to speak against my servant Moses?"* Numbers 12:9 goes on to say, *"the anger of the Lord burned against them."*

The result was God harshly chastising Miriam and Aaron, striking Miriam with leprosy. Even after Moses prayed and asked God to forgive his siblings and heal his sister, God still demanded Miriam be kept outside the camp alone for seven days. God was *not* happy with what they had done.

There are many more examples like this of how God takes it very personally when people do or say things which cause damage to His church and/or its leaders. In both the Old Testament and New, therefore, we see God sometimes choosing to take action against those who do damage to His church for their own selfish pursuits. In some of these cases, *people may even be deceived into believing they are doing the right thing for the right reasons* but are simply ignorant about the matters we will discuss in more detail in subsequent chapters.

The previous statement regarding God taking action against those who do damage to His church may turn your theology on its head, but it's right there in the Bible, right? It's pretty black and white. It was true of God in the Old Testament, and it's true of Him in the New. Even if God doesn't do the cursing, we can certainly conclude with accuracy that a process of sowing and reaping has been set in place with the actions people take.

More on this concept in the next chapter.

3

The Inescapable Process
of Sowing and Reaping

Galatians 6:7 is a verse many people know well:

> *Do not be deceived: God is not mocked,*
> *for whatsoever one sows, that will he also*
> *reap.* (ESV)

An example from my own life clearly illustrates this truth.

Many years ago, my wife and I were the worship leaders at a church in our region. The church was pastored by a man of God who we were very close to. He had sown much into us and was and is a man of great integrity. We had agreed to come back to his church after leaving once before very abruptly because of a terrible relational fallout in the worship ministry that was not getting any better, but only worse. We were gone for two years and had later agreed to come back temporarily to participate in an extended training series they were doing which my wife Donna and I were interested in. While we were there, we agreed to lead the worship ministry, which was still struggling since our departure. We agreed to stay on for six months and train someone else to take our place and then move on to a church closer to our home in Greenwood, Indiana, an hour away.

Donna and I labored diligently for those six months, but no one emerged who had the skill set to train to take over for us. So we labored on. Six months turned into a year, and a year turned into three years! We were there for Wednesday evening services and Thursday night rehearsals. We were there very early before Sunday School, which required us to get up about 6:00 a.m. on Sunday mornings to make 8:00 a.m. rehearsals. We were also there for Sunday evening services. On Sundays our practice was to drive down to Elizabethtown, Indiana very early, and then stay at our pastor's house afterward or hang out in town all day and wait for Sunday evening services because our home was so far away. We couldn't easily drive home and then come back for Sunday evening services. Even though we were young and more energetic, we were getting exhausted! Our little family of four was suffering.

The nail in the coffin was when the leadership of the church decided to add a Saturday night service for the people who worked on Sundays or who preferred a Saturday night meeting. We then had to travel to Elizabethtown on Saturday afternoons, run a quick rehearsal before service, play the service, and then spend the night in a nearby hotel with our two small children so we wouldn't have to drive all the way home, and then be ready for the Sunday morning service the next day. The Saturday evening thing lasted only about 90 days before we were totally spent.

Donna and I labored in prayer about what to do, and we *thought* we heard God speaking to us to make our way out and relocate our family to a different church near our home in Greenwood. But take note of this very important principle:

It is never a good idea to make a major decision when you are very fatigued, frustrated, angry, offended, or sad. If you do, you will most often miss it. And it is also not a good idea to make a decision based solely on your own need or benefit, because Philippians 2:4 says to *"look not only to your own interests, but also the interests of others."*

We were very fatigued and just wanted some relief, and in that situation, emotions can sometimes speak louder than God's voice. The Holy Spirit's voice is described in the Word as a still, small voice, and discomfort can sometimes drown out that voice if we aren't careful. What people often think is God speaking to them is really just the strength of their own discomfort, fatigue or emotions.

In retrospect, the wise and honorable thing for Donna and me to do would have been to arrange a meeting with our pastor and say something along the lines of, "Can we please talk about how to scale down our responsibilities so we can keep going for the long haul? We can't keep this pace and do all these services for very much longer. Can we restrict our services to just Sunday mornings and Wednesday nights?" But we never even thought about having such a conversation, because by the time we reached the breaking point we were so fatigued that I now believe our ability to reason and hear from God was impaired. **This is what stress and fatigue does to you. It impairs your reason, your senses, and your judgment. It often alters your ability to discern accurately and hear from God clearly.**

When Donna and I spoke to our pastor about our desire to move on, for some reason he didn't think of other options to offer us, either. He accepted our resignation, even though he knew and we knew it was going to leave a significant hole in the church and damage the worship ministry.

The result? A few people eventually left the worship ministry and his church because they no longer enjoyed the worship as much. Shallow, but true. And us? We bounced around from church to church for a long time and were never able to land anywhere that felt like home. It was like we had become Nomads ourselves, spiritual vagabonds with no place to settle and call our home.

Years later, when God called us into our own ministry, eventually the ways we damaged His church and hurt His leaders in the past became crystal clear. And, boy, did we ever reap what we sowed! What we did to our former pastor was done to us many times over. People in important ministry roles left without warning and without good reasons. People who we thought were friends abandoned us like dogs with rabies over very petty, small things.

I must acknowledge the healthy tension between the concept of God punishing people for sin and the natural consequences flowing out from the law of sowing and reaping. On the one hand we do see that God severely punished Ananias and Sapphira, as discussed in the previous chapter. On the other hand, we know punishment for sin was poured out on Jesus when He hung on the cross as a substitute for your sins and mine. Perhaps what differentiates the two is motive. Even when people have pure motives, as Donna and I did in our previous church, universal laws are nevertheless set in motion with our sowing, whether it be wise or foolish choices.

For example, although God loves you and Jesus has paid for your sins, this will not stop gravity from pulling you swiftly to the ground if you get too close to the edge of a tall building and accidentally slip off. God set a universal law in place called the Law of Gravity, and you violate it to your own harm and perhaps even the harm of others if you happen to land on top of someone! You may have the best of intentions and may not intend to do any harm to yourself or others when you flirt with the edge of the building. But the inconvenient truth is a law was tampered with, and you and others pay the price for universal laws being violated. It isn't

God punishing people for violating universal laws. It is people's own foolishness that punishes them.

Although Donna and I thought we did the right thing for the right reasons and in a respectable time frame and honorable fashion when we left our former pastor's church, we nevertheless left him in a terrible spot with respect to the worship ministry. Yes, we kept our word to stay for six months, and even stayed much longer. Yet we still left a gaping hole when we departed. We damaged God's church without allowing for an opportunity to adjust what we were doing so we could keep up. We didn't mean anyone any harm, but we set a process in motion according to the law of sowing and reaping.

Now let's get back to Ananias and Sapphira.

Let's keep in mind that Ananias and Sapphira were not irreligious people who disdained God and His church. No, like Donna and me, they loved the church. After all, they loved it enough to sell some property and give a significant portion of the proceeds to the church they had become a willing part of. Let's also consider that the couple thought they were *benefiting* the church. They were doing a benevolent act, and their money would help the church. Yet in spite of the good intentions of Ananias and Sapphira, God *despised* their act. Why? **God judged their gift because of a partially self-serving motive.** They outright lied to the church leaders, which God said very clearly was the same as bald face lying to the Holy Spirit. ***What you do to God's church, you do to God.***

This is a very serious matter to consider. We had better be sure every act, every word, and every intention toward God's church is pure and not tainted with self-serving motives. Let's therefore borrow from the principle taught in the account of Ananias and Sapphira and apply it to the modern church setting.

A lot of people serve God on "my" terms. They will serve the church if it is comfortable or convenient, or if it's not too much work or effort, or if it doesn't cost them too much. Donna and I have always been of the mindset to go above and beyond in our work for the Kingdom. The *me-focus* so many people suffer from in the church is something I have therefore never been able to understand. Aside from a spirit of laziness and apathy, however, there are also those who do *damage* to God's church with their actions, even if they think their motives are pure or justified.

This is something I have had to soberly come to terms with myself, because so often as a pastor I have wanted to quit, even though I know doing so would leave collateral damage and hurt people, thus hurting God and His church. In fact, it just so happens that what God spoke to my heart that morning on July 20th, 2017 was given me just days after I had reached my lowest point in ministry and actually did have it my heart to close the doors of the church. So God dealt with me personally on this point, for sure. The tendency to quit and run out on what God started in one's life is true on both sides of the pulpit.

My experience has been if a person has in mind to move out of one church and into another across town, one-hundred percent of the time they fall back on the default line, "God told me," or "God is leading me out." *Yes, one-hundred percent of the time!* But does God lead people out of the church where He planted them and leave a significant hole in doing so, and damage one church for the sake of another? I submit to you, NO! God does not operate this way, unless, of course, one church is in great apostasy and error and the church leaders are in grave sin and will not repent. Other than that, *Jesus doesn't do damage to His own Bride!* God loves His Church and wants each and every church to do well, to prosper in their work, and to be well-manned and funded. God is not in the business of speaking to people and leading them out of one church and into another when the church they are leaving is very dependent on their service and their absence would place significant pressure or added workload on the pastor or other people or leave a gaping hole which cannot be filled at all.

> **God always has in mind your *long-term* benefit, but your long-term benefit will often mean you will need to sacrifice short-term comfort.**

Let's do as Jesus did and use a modern-day example to illustrate this in parable form.

Let's imagine you open a business, and you hire people to fill all the spots needing to be filled to make the business run smoothly and prosper.

Let's say your business begins to flourish and you open multiple locations. Then one day you decide you need to make some moves and shake things up, so you decide to relocate a high-profile manager who has helped to make his district prosper. In doing so, however, you leave a gaping hole in the one location without knowing how you are going to fill his spot, or with who. In short, you have sacrificed the productivity of one location for the sake of another.

Any savvy businessperson would tell you that a business owner who operates that way won't be in business very long. A skilled businessman would place the appropriate people where they are best utilized and move them only if they have another capable person to fill their spot.

Is God any less intelligent, then? Does He sacrifice the productivity of one faithful church for the sake of another?

Some people might say, however, "This move is what I believe is best for me and my family."

Listen, as difficult as this may be to grasp, and as much as it violates our Americanized version of me-centered Christianity, life in Christ is not just about what is immediately beneficial to you and your family. We must always consider how God's Kingdom works, and God always has in mind your *long-term* benefit, but your long-term benefit will often mean you will need to sacrifice short-term comfort. In doing so, the acid test question must always be asked: "How will this decision affect others?" We must always consider how our actions will affect someone else, and how it affects God's church according to the command of Philippians 2:4:

> *"Do not merely look out for your own personal interests, but also for the interests of others." (NAS)*

Living with Eternity in Mind

Speaking of looking out for the interests of others, some people easily pull up roots and leave the church they have been connected to for years when they feel there is a deficiency that is no longer meeting a certain desire or need of the family, or if the church is weak in a certain area of ministry or community service. What they fail to comprehend is when people identify deficiencies in their churches, it is probably because God intends for them to roll up their sleeves and help meet those needs. This is likewise true of a new church someone might be considering planting themselves in. But, alas, this never dawns on most folks, either because they don't want to work that hard, or because they are simply ignorant about these matters and are conditioned to treat church like any other product or service they consume and then discard. Thus, they wish only to serve on *their* terms, and are often not willing to reciprocate the service of their church by breaking a sweat in return. The mindset is, "God is leading me to leave my ministry position because my church has some deficiencies, so I'll leave and find a church that already has it all together to my liking." As a result, people often leave a ministry post in a church which desperately needs them for a different church that doesn't.

This is an unfortunate mindset because not only do people further cripple the churches they leave due to the loss of important ministry workers, but they also forfeit opportunities to sow good seeds and reap future rewards.

Revelation 21:4 tells us God will wipe away our tears in the New Jerusalem. I wonder, though, why there would be any tears at all once God is dwelling among His people and all things are put in order. I wonder if there will be tears in heaven due to people realizing the rewards that could have been theirs had they been faithful to what God called them to do, had they not

When people identify deficiencies in their churches, it is probably because God intends for them to roll up their sleeves and help meet those needs.

been so self-centered, and had they only been willing to deny themselves a little comfort once in a while in order to help shore up weak areas in their churches. Could this be what the Apostle Paul was talking about when he wrote to the Corinthian Christians?

> ***¹⁰By the grace God has given me, I laid a foundation as a wise builder, and someone else is building on it. But each one should build with care. ¹¹For no one can lay any foundation other than the one already laid, which is Jesus Christ. ¹²If anyone builds on this foundation using gold, silver, costly stones, wood, hay or straw, ¹³their work will be shown for what it is, because the Day will bring it to light. It will be revealed with fire, and the fire will test the quality of each person's work. ¹⁴If what has been built survives, the builder will receive a reward. ¹⁵If it is burned up, the builder will suffer loss but yet will be saved—even though only as one escaping through the flames.***
> **-1 Corinthians 3:10-15** (NIV)

Scripture clearly says people will suffer loss of reward in heaven, a concept I will elaborate on further in a later chapter. Could it be that when people experience this loss, they will shed tears the Father will then wipe away as He showers us with His glorious presence and love? No one knows for certain what this scene will look like, but it's clear that even the works of Christian people will be judged and rewards will be given to the deserving while others will experience loss of reward. Those experiencing loss will still be saved but may nevertheless feel the weight of what could have been theirs for all eternity.

I do not intend to heap any guilt or condemnation on those who have failed in the past in areas of faithfulness because I myself have failed in this way. God is gracious and there is forgiveness. Nevertheless, this is a weighty matter to consider, and we can prevent further loss of reward if we make some adjustments.

To Everything There is a Proper Timing

Ecclesiastes 3:1 says there is a time for everything and a proper season for every activity under heaven.

If severing yourself from a ministry hurts the church you are leaving and impairs its ability to function as God intends because there is no one to fill your spot, then I submit to you based upon what we have seen in God's Word that this is not the will of God. God does not shoot Himself in the foot. Again, God has good administrative sense. He will not intentionally damage one church for the sake of another.

Therefore, our decisions to leave any ministry where God has planted us needs to bear this in mind. If you fill an important ministry role in your church and feel God is leading you out for whatever reason, and if God has provided a suitable replacement for you who makes your departure seamless, fine. But even if you are absolutely certain God spoke to you about leaving, a proper time of waiting for the appropriate time for God to raise up your replacement should be adhered to.

It reminds me of now-famous pastor, Keith Moore, who used to work under the late Kenneth Hagin. About ten years into Keith's service to Pastor Hagin, he felt God was calling him into his own ministry. Yet he did not run right out and launch his own ministry, leaving Pastor Hagin in a difficult spot. Nor did he jockey to do things *his* way in Pastor Hagin's ministry. He knew he would get to forge his own ministry in his own style someday. He therefore simply waited for the proper timing. In fact, he waited and waited and waited until God put everything in order. He waited for another ten years! When he did finally launch out on his own, it was like God shot him out of a cannon! His ministry catapulted seemingly overnight to international status and influence. Keith Moore did things right in the proper time and with a high degree of honor, thinking not just of himself but also the interests of others. And God greatly rewarded him for it.

Keith Moore's experience is much like young David when Samuel anointed him king. David had just been called in from the field to be presented before Samuel when he was anointed. He was probably sweaty, dirty and smelled like sheep. After he was anointed, he most likely turned right back around and walked back into the fields to resume his work. Why? Because that's all he could do. His time had not yet come. While the vision had been placed in his heart, he had to be faithful to what was set before him during the present season while he waited for the next one to materialize.

I will close this chapter with a quote from Rick Renner's excellent book, *Turning Your God-Given Dreams into Reality*. He writes,

> "I believe in the law of sowing and reaping as one of the basic principles of life. Galatians 6:7 teaches that what you *sow*, you will *reap*. If you want to reap glorious results from the dreams God has placed in your heart, you will have to sow some seeds to give birth to those dreams and then nurture them to maturity in your life.
>
> This is why I highly recommend the following: If you don't yet know how to get started on fulfilling *your* dream, you should get involved in helping someone else fulfill *his* dream. What you do for others will come back to you. *That's one aspect of the law of sowing and reaping.*
>
> It is important that you take advantage of this preparation time in your life. Use it as a season to invest in your own future by sowing seeds into someone else's future. Those seeds of being a blessing to someone else will eventually come back to you as a harvest of blessings in your own life, ministry, or business."

4

What if You are Being Tested?

Thomas Carlyle said, *"Permanence, perseverance and persistence in spite of all obstacles, discouragements, and impossibilities: It is this, that in all things distinguishes the strong soul from the weak."*

The strong soul versus the weak. That resonates with me. I want to strive toward having a strong soul and not a weak one. How about you? Unfortunately, far too many people in our society and even the church are defined by weakness of soul because they are unwilling to "endure hardship as a good soldier of Jesus Christ," to quote the Apostle Paul (see 2 Timothy 2:3). Today's shallow, me-centered culture has very little tolerance for discomfort. Instant gratification rules our society, and the younger the person the more pronounced this tendency seem to be. Practically gone are the days when people understood and practiced delayed gratification for future reward. I heard pastor Keith Moore once say that while our society preaches "get it now anyhow," God's methods are, "if you'll wait, it'll be great."

Unfortunately, the church in America leans toward the instant gratification camp over the delayed gratification camp. "My way or the highway" seems to rule the day. If you want to be blessed beyond measure, however, God says in so many words, "It's MY way, not *your* way."

God's people in America today largely do not recognize one of God's primary methods of refining His people and chiseling their character, which is often placing them in uncomfortable or undesirable situations at times, requiring them to be diligent, trustworthy, and honorable even in situations where they would like nothing better than to escape.

David, as an example, had the opportunity to kill the murderous King Saul and assume the throne rightfully his. David had already been anointed as the next king, and in that time and place no one would have faulted David or held him guilty for hastening the process by killing a madman king who had literally become so demon possessed that he once killed 70 priests and their entire families simply because they helped David as he fled for his life. In fact, on the two occasions where God put Saul into David's hands and his men urged him to end the king's life, David would not do it, stating he would "not touch the Lord's anointed." David therefore continued running from Saul and waited for God's timing for another 13 years!

What an honorable heart David had! What character! What nobility! Rather than taking the road of instant relief by taking matters into his own hands even as he was leading the terrible life of a fugitive, David waited on God, even though circumstances indicated it was God Himself Who arranged for Saul to fall into David's hands. Yes, it was indeed God Who arranged that, but it was not for the purpose of ending Saul at the hands of David. It was not for the purpose of ending David's undesirable circumstances immediately. Rather, it was for the purpose of testing David's heart.

Let me say it another way.

When circumstances indicated that God had placed David in a situation which required him to act, things were not as they seemed. Although the people around David were counseling him on what they interpreted as the will of God, it wasn't

> **God's people in America today largely do not recognize one of God's primary methods of refining His people and chiseling their character, which is often placing them in uncomfortable or undesirable situations of some sort, requiring them to be diligent, trustworthy, and honorable even in situations where they would like nothing better than to escape.**

God leading David to kill Saul at all. Rather, on those two occasions where killing Saul seemed like the most reasonable thing to do, *David was being tested!* Against the imploring of his men who were also leading the lives of fugitives, David refused to give into their urging. Why? Because David knew what was honorable. He knew instant gratification leads to consequences while delayed gratification for the sake of doing the honorable thing leads to reward.

And, boy, did David ever pass the test! As a result, David went down in history as the most respected and the most beloved King in Israel's history, "a man after God's own heart." God indeed took care of both Saul and David according to what they deserved in *His* time, and the outcome was better than what David could have produced himself.

In contrast to David's response to delayed destinies, let's turn our attention to Abraham and Sarah. They, too, had a delayed destiny. God had promised the barren couple a son, but year after year dragged by and there was no sign their situation was going to be any different. Understandably, they began to get impatient, even desperate. After several years of waiting, the couple attempted to bring about a son their own way. Sarah's not-so-brilliant idea was to give her handmaiden, Hagar, to Abraham as a stand-in of sorts and have a son by proxy. Hagar indeed conceived and bore a son, but it did not work out like anyone had hoped. Relations became so strained that Sarah couldn't stand it and actually blamed Abraham for the trouble. The couple's attempt to bring about the will of God their own way resulted in heartbreak when Abraham eventually sent away his own son, Ishmael, along with Hagar. Ishmael has affected the whole world in a very negative way ever since, thousands of years later, as he grew up to be the founder of a religious system which later evolved into what is now known as Islam. The consequences of moving out ahead of God and doing things one's own way can affect generations!

Let's now apply the lesson of the contrasting examples of David and Abraham to the situation in which you now find yourself. Perhaps it's undesirable. Maybe the arrival of your personal Promised Land seems delayed, and it is tempting to take matters into your own hands and act. Perhaps like Abraham and Sarah you're chomping at the bit to move forward, and there seems to be a logical and "spiritual" way out.

But what if you're being tested?

What if there is a reward up ahead God wants to lavish on you and a calling He wants to eventually bring you into, but He has to chisel your character before you can get there? What if the discomfort you are in is exactly where God wants you right now? This is why it says in James 1:2-4,

> *²Consider it all joy, my brethren, when you encounter various trials, ³knowing that the testing of your faith produces endurance. ⁴And let endurance have its perfect result, so that you may be perfect and complete, lacking in nothing.* (NAS)

Did you catch that? The *testing of your faith! Various trials! Endurance!* It all works together. You cannot get to the "*lacking in nothing*" part without the endurance.

And you can't get to the endurance part without having to exercise it in the midst of various trials which vex you.

> **What if there is a reward up ahead God wants to lavish on you and a calling He wants to eventually bring you into, but He has to chisel your character before you can get there? What if the discomfort you are in is exactly where God wants you right now?**

Samuel Johnson said perceptively, *"Great works are performed not by strength but by perseverance."*

I'm convinced God will orchestrate certain situations in believers' lives where they are forced to exercise perseverance and patience. When they pass the test and persevere through various trials, God then has a legal right to bless certain people more than others! **No one can ever accuse God of unfairly lavishing blessing on some people more than others because the tests certain people pass give Him that right which no one can challenge.**

God may want people to stay in certain situations for a time even though it is uncomfortable because He has something He wants to teach them, some character He wants them to develop, and some flesh He wants to kill! If people abort this process, however, they have to take a re-test somewhere else.

You see, when people bail out on God's chiseling process, they will get relief momentarily and all will seem great for a little while because they are out from under the heat of the refining fire. But after some time, they find themselves right back in the heat of the fire again. As the saying goes, "Out of the frying pan, into the fire." They don't understand why they go around the same mountains over and over again and can't seem to make significant progress. ***It's because they are trail jumpers!*** God has them on one trail, and as soon as it gets rocky, they jump the trail. Then God lovingly leads them through other methods, eventually getting them back onto a similar path, and as soon as they hit a rocky patch again, they find "spiritual" reasons to once again jump the trail. And around and around the mountain they go!

Some people never do learn to submit to God's chastening process. As soon as a situation gets uncomfortable or goes differently than they think it should they pull up roots again and relocate, and they forfeit the growth and blessing process God has in mind. Many of God's people today do not understand what chastening is for and what God is trying to accomplish. Whether the chastening be in the form of correction from a spiritual overseer, or a circumstance of some sort God is using to refine you (such as being under the authority of a difficult person and having to remain godly throughout the process, such as was the case with young David under King Saul), chastening is always for our good and is preparation for the assignment God has in mind for the future if we submit ourselves to it and learn from the experience.

The Greek word for *chastening* in many instances is not linked to a spanking, but rather implies child training, as a parent lovingly guides and disciplines a child. Yet many people refuse to be rooted enough to ever persevere through that loving process. And yes, it *is* a loving process.

Christianity 101

Please understand that perseverance through trial is Christianity 101. It represents the *basics* of life in Christ.

Think of it this way: If you want to get your physical body in shape, it's good to eat right, but this is only part of the picture. You need to apply some resistance to your muscles in the form of physical exercise. When it comes to your spiritual health, the Word of God is your food, but persecution, pressure, and problems provide the opportunities for you to exercise what you have learned in the Word of God. It's great to read about forgiveness, for example. However, until someone actually wrongs you and hurts you deeply, giving you the opportunity to actually exercise forgiveness, you don't really know about forgiveness.

Life in Christ is not the easiest path for this reason. We will have countless opportunities to die to our flesh and choose to exercise what we know to be right and true. If life in Christ was a bed of roses, *everyone* would be living for Christ! The reason so many people turn away from the truth is because they know truth is going to cost them something. This is why Jesus said to take up your *cross* and follow Him. It's a constant death to self. But don't let this dying process discourage you. God promises rewards for those who do not give up when the pressure is the greatest.

> **And let us not be weary in well doing: for in due season we shall reap, if we faint not.**
> **-Galatians 6:9** (KJV)

I also like this quote from Newt Gingrich:

"Perseverance is the hard work you do after you get tired of doing the hard work you already did."

This is how it works in the church as well. God often plants people where He knows they will best be used and grow the most. As Robert Gay says in his superb book, *Planted*, God is a good gardener, and like any good gardener He will lovingly plant people in the kind of soil where He knows they will flourish and grow the best, but He doesn't leave it there. He will then at times apply some of that obnoxious-smelling fertilizer (manure) in order to stimulate better growth. So often, however, God's people don't like the fertilizing process. It's uncomfortable. It's "stinky." Rather to remain steadfast and see this process to its conclusion, most Christians these days, it seems, will pull up and move on to another garden that God did not ordain for them during those times where the pressure is on and progress seems stagnant. Thus, they pull up their roots and stunt their growth.

This is why Proverbs 3:3 instructs, **"let love and faithfulness never leave you."** That word translated into English as *faithfulness* is the Hebrew word, *emeth*, which means *firmness, reliability, stability, continuance, established.* It implies the firmness which comes from being planted and deeply rooted, not moved by negative circumstances, discomfort, or emotions.

Proverbs 3:3-4 goes on to provide the results of this kind of faithfulness:

> **³Let love and faithfulness never leave you; bind them around your neck, write them on the tablet of your heart. ⁴Then you will win favor and a good name in the sight of God and man.** (NIV)

Immovable faithfulness and firmness will win you favor with God and man!

Any good gardener knows if a plant is uprooted even once, you stunt the growth for a time. If the plant is uprooted too often, it dies. It is best for the plant to be planted and then remain, withstanding the heat, wind, and cold, and growing a deep root system and flourishing. Anyone skilled in husbandry (the care and cultivation of crops) will tell you the sweetest fruit are those that have withstood inclement weather. There is something about the pressure of surviving in turbulent times which makes the fruit sweeter. This is also true of the nutrient content in plants. Botanists know herbs and other plant foods that have withstood dry climates or other challenging weather conditions are the most nutrient dense.

I like this quote from an unknown source on the results of steadiness through trial: *"Those who have walked through the fire leave sparks of light everywhere they go."* This is one reason why our Lord Jesus so often paralleled agriculture with spiritual concepts in His parables. Plants and agriculture teach us about how God's Kingdom operates. It is this same language of agriculture that even the Psalmist used when he wrote,

> **¹²The righteous will flourish like a palm tree, they will grow like a cedar of Lebanon; ¹³_planted_ in the house of the Lord, they will flourish in the courts of our God. ¹⁴They will still _bear fruit_ in old age, they will stay _fresh and green_, ¹⁵proclaiming, "The Lord is upright; he is my Rock, and there is no wickedness in him."**
> **-Psalm 92:12-15** (NIV, emphasis added)

Notice again the agricultural references. This is not an accident. It is by design. The connotation of the word *planted* there means steadfast, constant, to remain, and immovable.

If you are in the midst of pressure, trial, disappointment, or unfulfilled longing, you could be in the exact place where Joseph, David, Moses, Paul and many others found themselves by the will of God. Don't uproot and bail out on God's refining and fertilizing process in you. It is important you remain steadfast when testing comes. Otherwise, you will just get to take a re-test in some other time and place. Pass the test *now*, in this season, and be promoted in God's time!

As Winston Churchill so perceptively said, *"If you are going through hell, keep going."*

5

The Vine and the Branches

As an avid reader there are many books which have provided wisdom for my life over the years. I have read dozens of books. I can count only a few, however, that have made an indelible impact on me and are on my list of must-reads, ones I will refer back to many times and even read over and over again. One of those books is Bruce Wilkinson's *Secrets of the Vine*, which I highly recommend as a supplement to this book.

Wilkinson's book is a masterful study of Jesus' words recorded in John 15. While I obviously cannot review this passage of Scripture to the extent Bruce Wilkinson did, I will nevertheless provide a few insights pertinent to our discussion.

Let's begin with the words of the Master, Jesus:

> [1]*"I am the true vine, and My Father is the vinedresser. [2]Every branch in Me that does not bear fruit He takes away; and every branch that bears fruit He prunes, that it may bear more fruit. [5]I am the vine, you are the branches. He who abides in Me, and I in him, bears much fruit. [8]By this My Father is glorified, that you bear much fruit."*
> **-John 15:1-2,5,8** (ESV)

Using the metaphor of the vineyard, Jesus introduced yet another agricultural parallel to help us understand our role in bearing fruit for God. Let's examine the primary components of the picture Jesus painted.

First, Jesus Himself is the vine. This is important because He is the central theme of the metaphor. Everything springs from Him.

Secondly, the Father is the vinedresser, or the gardener. The role of the vinedresser is key because it is the vinedresser who must find ways to maximize the yield from his vineyard. In other words, the vinedresser will nurture as much fruit as he can from his plants.

Thirdly, you and I are the branches. The branches are the focus of the vinedresser's labor because they produce the fruit He is after. The vinedresser lovingly cultivates each branch so they will bear the maximum amount of fruit.

Jesus' words bring to remembrance a passage in the Old Testament He undoubtedly knew well, as did any faithful Israelite.

> *¹Blessed is the man...²[whose] delight in is the law of the Lord, and on His law he meditates day and night. ³He shall be like a tree, planted by rivers of water, that brings forth its fruit in its season, whose leaf also shall not wither, and whatever he does shall prosper.*
> **-Psalm 1:1,3** (NKJV)

What sort of fruit is our Father, the Vinedresser, looking for? It begins with a change in our perspectives, in the way we think. Our thoughts and attitudes should begin shifting from self-serving motives and passions to becoming more others-focused and God-honoring. In short, it starts with a renewed a mind. In the words of the Apostle Paul in Romans 12:2,

> *Do not conform to the pattern of this world, but be transformed by the renewing of your mind. Then you will be able to test and approve what God's will is—His good, pleasing and perfect will.* (NIV)

This shift in thinking is a lifelong process, by the way. It is literally never complete. We will constantly need to adjust attitudes, behaviors, moods, and thought patterns in order to conform to the image of Christ. As we do, a natural outflow of a renewed mind is the fruit of good works – deeds done for the Kingdom both inside the church and outside of it. We are all called to be fruit-bearers in the world and fruit-bearers in the church, helping bring people into the Kingdom and playing roles in building up the Body of Christ in our local churches.

This fruit-bearing glorifies the Father, according to John 15:8. *"By this My father is glorified, that you bear much fruit,"* Jesus said.

Jesus' point in providing this metaphor was not lost on the disciples, who lived in that agricultural society

> **Our thoughts and attitudes should begin shifting from self-serving motives and passions to becoming more others-focused and God-honoring.**

and who undoubtedly were picturing the baskets of grapes that vineyards yield as Jesus spoke.

In a nutshell, Jesus was saying to the disciples of that time and this:

Each child of God is a branch designed to produce fruit, and since different ones of us are producing fruit at different levels, the Father, the Vinedresser, will step in to help us produce more fruit. Some people, just like grapevines, are producing no fruit. Others are producing a little. Some Christians are producing good amounts of fruit and still others are producing an abundance. In each case, the Father wants more fruit because more fruit is always possible. He therefore tends us to help us continue moving toward abundance.

You Were Created for Abundance

You were created for abundance, but if you don't know and apply Jesus' vineyard teachings, you will never experience the abundant life you have been longing for. If you think perhaps your branch shows little or no fruit, then there are obviously some truths you need to work in your heart more deeply about the Vinedresser and His branches. In doing so, you may discover why you and other well-meaning and good-hearted believers get stuck in pain, turmoil, want, vicious cycles, and fruitlessness.

This is important to our discussion on serving with honor because when you understand the metaphor of the vine and the branches it will suddenly dawn on you why things may have happened the way they have in your life and ministry, and this understanding will transform your thinking about your service.

The first thing we must understand in reaching the destination of abundance is that a vinedresser *prunes* the branches in order to stimulate more growth. What does this look like?

Professional vinedressers know vines have a tendency to favor the growth of the vines themselves often at the expense of the fruit. There is sometimes so much growth of the wood from the branches that it crowds out the sun and moisture from getting to the buds and the grapes, thus hindering the growth of the fruit. An experienced vinedresser is happy to see growth, but what he is ultimately looking for is abundant fruitfulness. So out come the shears, and he begins cutting back some of the wood in order to stimulate growth of the fruit.

Remember, Jesus didn't use this metaphor for nothing. There was purpose and meaning for the believer in His comparison to us as branches. God the Father, our Vinedresser, will prune His children in order to stimulate more growth. Pruning always involves cutting back and cutting away that which is useless, and then lifting up out of the dirt that which is useful and desired so it will flourish. Let's look at Jesus' words again.

> *"Every branch in Me that does not bear fruit He takes away* [cuts off]*; and every branch that bears fruit He prunes* [lifts up]*, that it may bear more fruit."*

Notice He cuts off branches not bearing fruit, and branches bearing *some* fruit He prunes in order to stimulate even more growth.

You might be in a pruning season in your life right now. It may seem as though you have been downsized, restricted, confined, forgotten, or even shelved. But none of those things are true. God is always *for* you, not against you. He is always interested in your long-term fruitfulness, and long-term fruitfulness is often accomplished at the expense of short-term comfort.

Bruce Wilkinson said it well when he wrote,

> "God's strategy for coaxing a greater harvest out of his branches is not the one you and I would prefer. His plan is to prune, which means to thin, to reduce, to cut off. The principle of pruning invites a revealing question about your spiritual life: Are you praying for God's superabundant blessings and asking Him to make you more like His Son? If the answer is yes, then you are asking for the shears. Pruning is how God answers your prayers that your life will please Him more and have a greater impact for eternity."

Let me give you two examples of how the pruning process looks.

Moses probably felt like he had been downsized and restricted perhaps more than anyone in the Bible. He was the adopted son of Pharaoh's daughter, after all. He was a powerful person in Egypt, part of the royal family. He was rich, influential, and likely feared. When he sensed a call on his life to free the Hebrews, the people of his heritage, a series of events occurred that left him isolated in Midian, of all places, tending sheep, of all things. That was probably *not* Moses' idea of advancement in ministry! But God was pruning Moses. He was cutting off the dead things in Moses' life which had no eternal value. God was teaching him faithfulness and getting the culture of Egypt out of him so he could bear much fruit later – *later* being the word of emphasis here. In the life of Moses, *later* meant 40 years! He was 80 years old when his ministry began!

Don't be discouraged if things are moving along slower than you had hoped. It doesn't mean you are on the wrong track. In fact, it could very well mean you are on the right one! God may have you in Midian for a while before He can release you to greater fruitfulness.

Another example along these lines comes in the form of the more recent story of Christian music artist Lincoln Brewster.

> **Long-term fruitfulness is often accomplished at the expense of short-term comfort.**

Lincoln Brewster is almost a household name these days if you are part of a contemporary church that sings more modern-style worship songs. Lincoln Brewster has written many wonderful worship songs sung worldwide. He is also considered one of the world's finest guitarists. How did Lincoln Brewster get to the point of such abundant fruitfulness?

The backstory of Lincoln Brewster begins with his pre-Christian life as a guitarist in the secular world of rock music. When Steve Perry, the former lead singer for the platinum-selling rock group *Journey*, set out to pursue a solo career, Lincoln Brewster was his guitarist. Lincoln traveled and toured with Steve Perry for a few years, but then he got gloriously saved. That marked the end of Lincoln's career with Steve Perry because God pruned him, and Lincoln could therefore no longer in good conscience live that kind of life and pursue a passionate relationship with God at the same time.

God's pruning process in Lincoln Brewster's life was not restricted to quitting secular music, however. Having been associated with such big names in the music business, Lincoln Brewster could have easily used his former life as a platform to pursue "big" opportunities in the world of Christian music. But that's not what he did. As God's pruning process would have it, there was some pride and self-glorification God had to get out of Lincoln. He had to get "Egypt" out of him. In submission to God's pruning process, Lincoln Brewster found himself assisting the worship team in a very small church made up of mostly elderly people. (You can't tell me God doesn't have a sense of humor!) Still sporting hair down to his shoulders, Lincoln faithfully and humbly served that church and those people with his amazing guitar skills, although those skills were not really being highlighted to their fullest extent. He was faithful to what God put before him for that season of his life – steady, immovable, and constant. The rest is history. Lincoln Brewster, as already stated, is internationally known in the world of Christian music and his songs are sung in churches across the world every Sunday.

I'm convinced the Christian world would probably not know the name Lincoln Brewster had he not submitted to God's pruning process and shown himself faithful to the "small" things God gave him to do early in his Christian life and ministry.

A truth I wish every Christian could get a grasp of is that God couldn't care less about the size and scope of your ministry if your heart isn't right. And only God knows if your heart is ready for promotion in His Kingdom. It is for this reason He prunes people, to cut off or scale back things we don't even recognize need to be pruned. I wish every Christian would learn to not despise small or difficult beginnings, but to embrace them as God's pruning process.

If we could see up ahead the wonderful promotion God has in store for the faithful who don't give up when times get tough, we wouldn't complain about being in Midian.

> ***"No eye has seen, no ear has heard,***
> ***and no mind has imagined what God has***
> ***prepared for those who love Him."***
> **-1 Corinthians 2:9** (NLT)

6

"Dance with the One Who Brung Ya"

Have you ever heard the saying, "Dance with the one who brung ya?" It has the picture of a young man inviting a young lady to a dance or party, going out of his way to pick her up and paying for the evening and then taking her to the dance only to have her dance with other men. It's a wise old saying which speaks to the importance of loyalty toward those who have invested in you.

Proverbs 19:22 alludes to this as well. It says, **"What is desirable in a man is his fidelity."** The New Living Translation renders it like this: **"Loyalty makes a person attractive."**

God values loyalty, and He honors it.

This is one of the reasons why I believe I have been blessed in business, because I have always danced with the one who "brung" me. I have always been loyal in the business setting. When I was still young and inexperienced, the CEO and owner of a nutraceutical company saw something in me I didn't even see in myself. He believed in me, invested money in my educational process and trained me according to the principles he knew would help me – and thus him – to prosper. He was also patient with my long learning curve when I was undeveloped and my presentation skills were rough and clunky.

As a result of that investment in me I began to prosper in that business. As I did, other people began to take notice. I was later contacted by job recruiters in the pharmaceutical industry asking me if I would consider making a career move. One of the competing companies in my niche of the field reached out to me about job openings, and I can't count the number of times doctors have approached me about working in their clinics as a consultant or getting me involved in a marketing program. I never expressed interest in any of these opportunities, however, even though some of them looked attractive. Even during some lean years when the business seemed to be going south, I still did not leap over into supposedly greener pastures for the sake of escaping my circumstances. Why? Because it was my boss who invested in me, not one of these other people who just wanted to benefit from his time and expense. It was him who helped get me where I eventually went in my business, and therefore it was his company and his interests I aligned my heart to. I have considered my job as an assignment from God and my boss as an extension of God's authority. My role is to bless my boss and do my job the way *he* wants it done. God has blessed me because of that sense of loyalty.

My boss and I have not always seen eye-to-eye, however. He has made me angry at times. There are times I wished he would have done things differently. But I figure if I was smart enough to run a business like his it would be me in that position and not him. In spite of our differences in some areas my loyalty to him has remained steadfast until which time it is obvious a move out would benefit both him and me equally, because I am looking out for not only my own interests, but also his.

You see, being a student of Proverbs since my late twenties I read and obeyed a passage of Scripture many years ago that has benefited me in business ever since.

> ***The one who guards a fig tree will eat its fruit, and whoever protects their master will be honored.***
> **–Proverbs 27:18** (NIV)

The New Living Translation renders it like this:

> ***As workers who tend a fig tree are allowed to eat the fruit, so workers who protect their employer's interests will be rewarded.***

I have always tried to live by that. I have tried to never just think of myself when it comes to my relationship with those over me. I wish I could say this was always true of the past ministry positions I was in, but I've learned along those lines, too. Loyalty to those who have invested in you to help make you what you are today is a very, very important principle to God, and it should be to us. It's a principle of honor, which God esteems highly but which our culture now knows very little.

Even though this verse in Proverbs is speaking mostly of a business relationship between an employer and an employee, or even a master and a slave such as was the case with loyal and faithful Joseph in Egyptian slavery, we can see this principle at work even in relationships outside the realm of business.

For example, you may remember the story of when Abraham won a great military victory over an alliance of three kings and gained a huge amount of plunder. Scripture records in Genesis 14 that Abraham tithed from the plunder to Melchizedek the priest. This is significant, so pay close attention.

Who was Melchizedek? Theories abound. Some say he was the pre-incarnate Christ. Maybe so. A historical book of the time suggests something else, however. The ancient book of Jasher, which was a highly regarded historical record of the time (so highly regarded that it was referenced three times in the Bible), says Melchizedek was Noah's son Shem who later became a priest in that region where Abraham lived. When Abraham left his father's house and set out on his own, the book of Jasher records he was taken in by Shem and lived with him for a time, and Shem taught Abraham the ways of the Lord.

In response to Shem's investment in him, Abraham felt it was loyal and honorable to give back to his spiritual overseer and father in the faith.

This is a theme seen all throughout Scripture. Loyal and honorable people like Joseph, David, Daniel, and many others never ran out on those who invested in them even when staying put was not desirable. There are, however, people in Scripture who did not choose the path of honor and loyalty. The grim outcome of their choices serves as warnings.

Here are three examples:

There was a young man by the name of John Mark who was one of the Apostle Paul's ministry partners. After casting his allegiance to Paul and his ministry, John Mark set out on a missionary journey with Paul only to abandon him and go back home when things didn't pan out to his liking. Later, John Mark changed his mind again and wanted to rejoin Paul and Barnabas on another missionary journey. But Paul refused. Paul no longer trusted John Mark because the young man had not shown himself faithful. Paul wanted people he could depend on, not deserters who changed with the tides.

Another example is found in the book of Philemon. Philemon was a businessman and owned slaves, or what might be better described as household servants. He had a servant named Onesimus who ran away. In Paul's letter to Philemon, he did not excuse the actions of the runaway slave. Instead, he acknowledged it was the right thing to do for Onesimus to return to Philemon. By this time Paul had become fond of Onesimus, who had become an important part of Paul's ministry. As Paul said in Philemon 1:13, *"I would have liked to keep him with me… but I did not want to do anything without your consent."*

The backstory is important to understand the significance of Paul's position in this situation.

Onesimus came into the faith as a result of Paul's ministry. Philemon, too, was Paul's son in the faith from some time earlier. Yet Paul did not demand anything from Philemon in the situation with Onesimus because Paul understood the importance of things done honorably and with a high degree of integrity and loyalty. He therefore appealed to Philemon to receive Onesimus back now as a friend and brother in Christ.

Take note: Even though Onesimus had now been separated from Philemon for a long time, and even though Onesimus had now come into the faith and was now Paul's faithful ministry partner on whom he had come to rely, Paul knew it was the right thing to do for Onesimus to go back and fulfill his duty to Philemon. It was going to cost Paul an important ministry partner to send Onesimus back, but he knew it was the honorable thing for them both to do in order to represent Christ's interests in a spirit of integrity. Onesimus obviously consented to this even though he knew he was likely going to be placed back into the role of a slave. Honor and loyalty were upheld.

On this point, I feel it is important to point out that Paul also appealed to Philemon on the basis of what he felt Philemon "owed" him. He wrote,

> *8"That is why I am boldly asking a favor of you. I could demand it in the name of Christ because it is the right thing to do. 9But because of our love, I prefer to simply ask you... 19And I won't mention that you owe me your very soul!"*
> **-Philemon 1:8,9,19** (NLT)

Because of the role he played in Philemon's spiritual conversion and discipleship, Paul obviously felt there was a certain amount of obligation Philemon owed him. While Paul did not make any demands on the basis of this obligation, he was careful to at least mention it so Philemon would not forget that debt.

Similarly, then, there should be a sense of obligation and loyalty toward those who have invested in us and who God has connected us to, especially if there was significant spiritual benefit derived from that relationship.

The third example on the importance of loyalty – and it is perhaps the most striking example of all – is that of Lot, Abraham's nephew. Again, the backstory is important to understand the point.

Before God changed his name when Abraham was still known as Abram, Lot had come into Abram's clan as a young man and was now prospering alongside his uncle because of the blessing on Abram's life. Abram made Lot who he was. His guidance and wisdom benefited Lot greatly. When Lot began to prosper, his herds and flocks became so large that the regions where they were grazing could not contain both his flocks and Abram's massive number of animals. This predicament led to the herdsmen of both parties beginning to argue, so Abram made Lot an offer.

> *⁸ So Abram said to Lot, "Let's not have any quarreling between you and me, or between your herders and mine, for we are close relatives. ⁹ Is not the whole land before you? Let's part company. If you go to the left, I'll go to the right; if you go to the right, I'll go to the left."*
> **-Genesis 13:8-9** (NIV)

And how did Lot respond?

> *¹⁰ Lot looked around and saw that the whole plain of the Jordan toward Zoar was well watered, like the garden of the Lord, like the land of Egypt. (This was before the Lord destroyed Sodom and Gomorrah.) ¹¹ So Lot chose for himself the whole plain of the Jordan and set out toward the east. The two men parted company: ¹² Abram lived in the land of Canaan, while Lot lived among the cities*

of the plain and pitched his tents near Sodom. (NIV)

This is a point of monumental importance.

Even though Abram gave Lot the choice of land, Lot gave no honor to his uncle who had invested so much in him when making his decision. He chose the best land for himself and gave Abram what was left. And Abram honored his choice. But God didn't. God honored Abram for being gracious to Lot, but what became of Lot as a result of his choice?

Scripture doesn't mention Lot again until chapter 19 of Genesis. By this time Lot and his family were living inside the city of Sodom among that wicked culture. Because of the prayers of Abram (now called Abraham by this time), God sent angels to remove Lot from Sodom before destroying it. Nevertheless, here is where we see how the consequences of Lot's decision to separate from Abraham the way he did become apparent.

Now removed from the blessing connected to Abraham, Lot's selfish pursuits catch up with him. He ends up no longer living on the plains enjoying safe pasture, but now residing fully within the most wicked culture of that time. While still maintaining a degree of integrity and honor of God, still, the culture had affected him and his family more than he knew. When the homosexual men of the city approached Lot's door demanding he send out the "men" (angels) who were in Lot's house so they could rape them, Lot did something outrageous. In an effort to redirect attention off the angels (as if the angels couldn't take care of themselves), Lot actually offered his daughters instead to the perverse desires of the men of the town! Can you imagine?!

The angels succeeded in getting them all out before the city was destroyed, but Lot's wife too had more of Sodom in her than she realized. When she looked back longingly at the burning city in

> **There are sometimes terrible consequences associated with a lack of loyalty and looking out only for yourself without considering the welfare of others.**

direct disobedience to the command of God through the angels, God turned her into a pillar of salt.

In no time at all, Lot soon found himself hiding out in a cave with his two daughters, his fortunes gone, his home incinerated, and his wife and sons-in-law-to-be all slain.

To add insult to injury, his daughters feared they would never see civilization or humanity again because of their long isolation in that cave, and their fear led to something despicable. In a desperate attempt to carry on their family line, both daughters decided to do something so perverse that it demonstrates how much of the wickedness of Sodom had affected them as well. On consecutive nights, Lot's daughters got their father very drunk and took turns having sexual relations with him in the hopes of conceiving and having children. And conceive they did. Can you imagine his horror when Lot finally realized what had happened? Eventually, those incestuous sons, Moab and Ben-Ammi, became the patriarchs of two very wicked cultures, the Moabites and Ammonites, who were murderous, idol-worshiping pagans.

All this came about as the ultimate result of one terrible decision on Lot's part: taking the easy way out and looking only to his own interests without considering the welfare of the one who was over him and who had invested so much in him.

There are sometimes terrible consequences associated with a lack of loyalty and looking out only for yourself without considering the welfare of others.

7

Discerning God's Will in Leaving a Church

In my years as a pastor, I have seen many people come and go in our church. It is sad but true that churches in America lose on average about six percent of their overall membership every year. Our church has been no different. Among all the people who have departed I can count on one hand those who have done it honorably and clearly in the will of God.

For some reason a very obvious truth concerning *basic* Christianity and life in Christ escapes many people when it comes to the various reasons they choose to leave churches. Scores of people are offended, frustrated over fixable things, and just plain selfish in why they choose to leave a church where God has planted them, and somehow they don't recognize it, or if they do, they refuse to acknowledge it.

On that note, let's examine a short passage of Scripture packed with hard-hitting truth.

> *"Make every effort to live in peace with everyone and to be holy; without holiness, no one will see the Lord."*
> **-Hebrews 12:14** (NIV)

The Greek word translated into English as "see" in that verse is, *horao*, which literally means *to see or perceive*. This verse could just as easily be translated like this: *Without holiness, no one will perceive the Lord.* I believe this is more consistent with the whole of Scripture. Those who do not live holy will not perceive the Lord's presence, His voice, or His direction.

Notice also the qualifier for holiness. This verse connects holiness to living at peace with everyone. Thus, we are commanded to *make every effort* to live in peace with all people since peace is connected to holiness and our holiness is connected to our discernment of God's presence, His will, and His voice.

What does it mean to live in peace with everyone? It must first be pointed out that some people may not want to live in peace with you, but that's between them and God. Where you and I are concerned, however, we must make every effort to harbor absolutely no hard feelings toward anyone, which is a tall order to be sure. If something is bothering us and we can't seem to get past it, the holy response is not to pretend it isn't there and then allow a root of frustration or bitterness to grow in our hearts. A person who concerns himself with living at peace with everyone goes to the person with whom he is having a problem and opens up to him in the hopes of resolving the problem and resuming a Christ-like relationship of love, transparency, and mutual trust and respect.

Going to a brother or sister who has offended you or with whom you are having a problem is not a suggestion. This is a command from our Lord when He said,

> *"If your brother or sister sins, go and point out their fault, just between the two of you. If they listen to you, you have won them over."*
> **-Matthew 18:15** (NIV)

With this command in mind, let's look again at Hebrews 12:14 and follow the logical progression of thought. If we make every effort to live in peace with everyone, this will contribute to our lives of holiness. If we live in holiness, we perceive the Lord and discern His will, direction, and voice. If we do not make every effort to live in peace with all people, however, then our lives are polluted and our holiness tainted. If our holiness becomes tainted through willful acts of shutting people out or harboring anger or hard feelings toward them, then we have cut ourselves off from the flow of God's Spirit and will fail to sense His direction and voice. Yet it is in this exact condition in which people choose to leave their churches: offended, frustrated, and refusing to communicate with those with whom they have issues. This is not and cannot be the will of God.

In his famous book and teaching series, *The Bait of Satan*, John Bevere said God told him there is only one way to leave a church, and it's according to Isaiah 55:12: ***You shall go out with joy and be led forth with peace.***

When people leave a church, it should only be because God is clearly leading them into a new chapter of their lives, and this sense should also be obvious to the pastor and congregation. That leading and sense of peace should also be accompanied by your role being filled by another capable person so things are not left in disarray when you depart. Since we are one Body, therefore, all parties should be able to discern the leading of the Spirit and celebrate the parting of ways without any sense that something is not right.

If a person cannot leave a church with an absolutely clear conscience that there is nothing between him and another person, without any degree of frustration or offense, without the honest-to-goodness blessing of the pastor, and without leaving a gaping hole in the departure, then *something is wrong*.

I love America, and it is because I love it that it is sad to me how we have become the land of the self-serving and the home of the independent. We Americans don't comprehend this concept of being connected to one another and operating as a body, as 1 Corinthians 12 teaches. A large portion of Western Christians tend to do pretty much whatever they want whenever they want to do it, still congratulating themselves for the avoidance of the "big" and more obvious sins. If they get restless and want to find another church, they do it, and they don't even think about the implications of that decision most of the time.

By contrast, Christians in other countries *do* understand this concept of body connectedness. In fact, a well-traveled pastor friend of mine explained to me how Christians in the north island of New Zealand understand and practice the Biblical principle of body connectedness very well. If a Christian there has the urge to leave a church, for example, that person always presents the urge to the pastor. If the pastor does not bear witness with the urging and declines to bless the departure, then most often the person will not leave until which time he or she can receive the full blessing of the spiritual overseer. *This is* how it's supposed to be done. Honor!

If a person cannot leave a church with an absolutely clear conscience that there is nothing between him and another person, without any degree of frustration or offense, without the honest-to-goodness blessing of the pastor, and without leaving a gaping hole in the departure, then *something is wrong.* A person who is interested in the blessing of God on his or her life cannot leave a church that way. It is clearly in direct violation of the Scriptures and the revealed will of God.

Commissioned

A friend of mine had a Kingdom encounter while on vacation a few years ago with a man named Brett. While at a conference my friend overheard Brett speaking to another person about ministry and decided to break in and introduce himself. In the ensuing conversation my friend learned that Brett was a missionary to Kenya as an extension of his home church. Brett described the details of his calling to my friend, explaining how one day someone vomited during one of their church services, and as Brett was cleaning up the mess suddenly his pastor pointed at him and said, "God is calling you out into the mission field."

That's most often how promotion in the Kingdom happens. It's a result of humble service to do whatever God puts before you now, and as you are faithful, He calls you out to do more.

The best and most honorable way to leave a church, therefore, is to be sent or commissioned by the leadership. In other words, one who is commissioned has been trained and mentored, and has arrived at a place spiritually and in one's ministry where he or she is now ready to function as an extension of that church in another location, such as a missionary or a church plant. The Apostle Paul's protégé, Pastor Timothy, as an example, was an extension of Paul's ministry. God always has reproduction in mind as a primary Kingdom priority, and so should we.

In some cases, a person may be legitimately called out of a church without being sent or commissioned. Sometimes people get relocated in their jobs and have to move out of State. In many cases these are legitimate reasons to leave a church. However, even in these cases a person with a *true* Kingdom mindset will inquire of the Lord with a willingness to give up a better career opportunity or a move to a different location for the sake of God's calling and assignment.

Some people will probably balk at such a suggestion, which demonstrates how worldly-minded we have become as a church culture. Staying in God's perfect will is always better in the long run compared to thinking only of monetary gain. God knows how to promote and prosper His faithful ones. But when the needs of God's Church are ignored for the sake of a job or a location, sometimes we may find the relocation was not what we had hoped. But even if it does end up being profitable in a temporal sense, we might never know what we missed out on in spiritual benefit and Kingdom promotion by being willing to take care of God's things before our own. We must walk by faith, not by sight.

For example, if leaving a church means the church will severely suffer in one's absence, then this question should be brought before the Lord: "What would *You* have me do, Lord? Do you want me to take this job, or stay and fill this need in my church for now?" Countless people in the Body of Christ would not even stop to pray about it if an attractive offer was waived in front of their faces. They would just pull up and move at a moment's notice if there is more money or a better location involved. The needs of God's church never cross their minds. In these cases, life is still all about *their* needs and wants because they have not yet learned to think like Kingdom people.

> **It is never a good idea to sit idle while you wait for your calling to unfold. In fact, that's the best way for it *not* to unfold. You must show yourself faithful to what God has set before you *now*. You must blossom where you are planted.**

In other situations, people might pull up and leave a church because of false teaching or unrepentant gross sin and/or spiritual abuse in the leadership. These are legitimate reasons to relocate. As already stated, however, on the occasions where this happens, God will most likely provide a replacement for the person leaving so the Biblical and godly church continues to function in a healthy manner. The only exception to this I have been able to find in Scripture is when a minister is sending someone who doesn't really belong to his ministry in the first place back to another ministry or person, such as was the case when the Apostle Paul sent Onesimus back to Philemon. Another exception might be in the case of leaving an apostate church.

Some people I know feel God has called them to a particular ministry of their own or a particular location to move to at some point, and they feel they should therefore not get involved in any church too deeply while they wait for those hopes and dreams to come to pass. Perhaps this is well-intentioned, but it is nevertheless a terrible mistake because if a person is unsure of the timing of such a move, he or she could be bearing fruit for the Kingdom while waiting for God to open the doors. It is never a good idea to sit idle while you wait for your calling to unfold. In fact, that's the best way for it *not* to unfold. You must show yourself faithful to what God has set before you *now*. You must blossom where you are planted. Then, perhaps, after a time you will be promoted and your calling will unfold, and you can be properly sent and commissioned by the leadership in your church rather than commissioning yourself.

Getting back to my days as a worship leader, God only knows what could have been if I had stayed put until which time I could be commissioned and sent out. My former pastor and I made a great team. But I got tired, frustrated, and impatient. I committed spiritual abortion. I aborted what God started. And I paid a price.

I believe God is making good use of my mistakes, however, by using me to teach other people how to avoid making the same mistakes, which is the reason for this book. I also believe God has in mind greater and greater degrees of fruitfulness for me (which is always His desire), but I have had to take a Joseph-like rerouting of the process. Perhaps I could have taken an easier route had I stayed the course at my previous church where I led worship. Who knows what would have happened as the years progressed. Perhaps I would have become an associate pastor and been trained and prepared more thoroughly prior to launching my own church, thus avoiding a lot of the mistakes I have made as a pastor. Or maybe I could have even enjoyed remaining an associate pastor and helping to hold up the arms of the man of God. There are all kinds of scenarios that could have come out of our relationship that I will probably never know about until I get to heaven. And it is there where God will wipe away my tears of regret.

Thank God for His mercy. He does allow restarts. He can work with our mistakes. Nonetheless, we can avoid many of those mistakes and speed up the process by applying Biblical wisdom.

As for you, you don't have to take the same road I took. You can take an easier, more streamlined route. Yes, you will still have to go through the same kind of waiting and preparation all great men and women of God have to endure, but at least you might prevent taking the circuitous "do-over" kind of route I have taken. Learn from one who has gone before, and don't make the same mistakes.

As has been said, "Those who do not learn from the past are destined to repeat it." Amen.

8

Receiving Your Full Reward

In First Peter 4:10, we are given a command for service.

> *Each of you should use whatever gift you have received to serve others, as faithful stewards of God's grace in its various forms.* (NIV)

Don't ever forget where your gifts and talents came from. They came from God, and they were given to you for the purpose of being given back to Him for use in His Kingdom. The Bible teaches that those who take up their crosses and serve Christ with the gifts, talents, and abilities which came from Heaven will receive a reward for their service.

In the parable of the talents in Matthew 25 Jesus told a story of a businessman who entrusted some of his money to three servants. A "talent" was a measure of money like dollars are today. The master entrusted different amounts of talents to each of the three according to their abilities. It is interesting to note that the money they received was not theirs; it was only given to them to invest on behalf of their master, and they would receive reward – or lack thereof – depending on how well they handled their master's property.

In the same way, God the Father has entrusted to each of His children some of His property in the form of abilities, talents, and even money, and He expects a return on that investment.

I know many Christians, especially artistic ones, who live as though their talents were given to them for the purpose of building their own kingdoms, bringing glory to themselves or scratching some personal itch. God does give His children abilities for their enjoyment and to provide for their families, but God also distributes His property to His people for the profit of His Kingdom as well. He is looking for fruitfulness, benefit to other people, and the personal value resulting from a lifestyle of service.

It is important to consider, however, that people who do indeed put their hand to the plow and contribute of their time, talents, and resources may nevertheless receive only a partial reward in the end. The Bible indicates there are different levels of reward in God's Kingdom. There are partial rewards for service, full rewards, and no rewards. This reward system has nothing to do with salvation itself, but the redeemed will receive rewards both in this life and in the one to come. The Apostle John further points out that we can lose some or all of our reward being stored up for us in eternity.

> **Watch out that you do not lose what we have worked so hard to achieve. Be diligent so that you receive your full reward.**
> **-2 John 8** (NLT)

It stands to reason that if there is a full-reward scenario, then there must also be partial reward and no reward scenarios. The Apostle John warned about the possibility of losing the reward for the things we have been working toward, so we should therefore be diligent to receive a *full* reward. This is related to what we discussed in chapter 3. The Apostle Paul wrote to the Corinthian Christians and explained that each person's work will be tested with fire, and some people will suffer loss and actually get into heaven with no reward.

People can be working diligently and spend much time, effort, and even money on building the Kingdom through their labor in the church and elsewhere, but they may receive only a partial reward for those efforts. Why? The answer is they are being unfaithful in certain areas, and God does not obligate Himself to bless unfaithfulness, as Scripture clearly communicates from Genesis 1 to Revelation 22.

Note the Apostle John writes in the aforementioned verse, "watch out." Another version says, "Look to yourselves." In other words, John encourages his readers of that time and this to *take heed and examine yourselves.* There is a soberness and urgency to his message not to be taken lightly. The reader is to ponder his words and examine oneself in light of the truth presented. His message is clear: *you can lose the reward laid up for you if you are not careful.*

Honoring Your Place

In pondering this point regarding the possibility of losing one's reward, let's read the parable of the talents in Matthew 25:14-30.

> **14For it is just like a man going on a journey, who called his servants and entrusted them with his possessions. 15To one he gave five talents, to another two talents, and to another one talent— each according to his own ability. And he went on his journey. 16The servant who had received the five talents went at once and put them to work and gained five more. 17Likewise, the one with the two talents gained two more. 18But the servant who had received the one talent went off, dug a hole in the ground, and hid his master's money.**
>
> **19After a long time the master of those servants returned to settle**

accounts with them. [20]The servant who had received the five talents came and presented five more. 'Master,' he said, 'you entrusted me with five talents. See, I have gained five more.'

[21]His master replied, 'Well done, good and faithful servant! You have been faithful with a few things; I will put you in charge of many things. Enter into the joy of your master!'

[22]The servant who had received the two talents also came and said, 'Master, you entrusted me with two talents. See, I have gained two more.'

[23]His master replied, 'Well done, good and faithful servant! You have been faithful with a few things; I will put you in charge of many things. Enter into the joy of your master!'

[24]Finally, the servant who had received the one talent came and said, 'Master, I knew that you are a hard man, reaping where you have not sown and gathering where you have not scattered seed. [25]So I was afraid and went out and hid your talent in the ground. See, you have what belongs to you.'

[26]'You wicked, lazy servant!' replied his master. 'You knew that I reap where I have not sown and gather where I

have not scattered seed. [27]Then you should have deposited my money with the bankers, and on my return I would have received it back with interest. [28]Therefore take the talent from him and give it to the one who has ten talents. [29]For everyone who has will be given more, and he will have an abundance. But the one who does not have, even what he has will be taken away from him. [30]And throw that worthless servant into the outer darkness, where there will be weeping and gnashing of teeth.' (NIV)

One servant apparently did not esteem what the master had entrusted to him. Perhaps he thought it was too small and insignificant since he only received one talent, whereas his fellow servants received much more. Therefore, he did not value his small amount and did nothing with it, hiding it in the ground so he could give it back to his master when he returned. Notice, however, how the master was displeased with the servant's lack of effort and failure to esteem what was entrusted to him. The master reprimanded and then punished the servant harshly. In so many words, the master said to the servant, *"I entrusted you with my property. I showed confidence in your ability to make a profit for me. But you did not value my confidence in you. You did not esteem what I entrusted to you. Therefore, what little you have will be taken away from you and given to someone who does value it."*

This is what happens all too often with the call of God on people's lives. I have witnessed people being honored with important ministry positions in the church only to watch them carelessly kick that position to the curb when they got offended, when things were not working out to their liking, when they got discouraged, or when they would not resist temptation and allowed themselves to get lured into gross sin.

My friends, this is shameful.

When the Master of the Universe shows confidence in you and places a calling on your life and starts you out with manning a certain post in the ministry, you are to honor and esteem your post. You should honor your place like you honor God, because that position came from His hand. If you want to receive a full reward, then nothing and no one should be able to talk you out of manning your post, because you are honoring the Commander-in-Chief Who trusted you with it. By doing so, you are likewise honoring the brethren who serve alongside you and who depend on you, and you esteem the post itself, whether a big role or a small one.

In manning your post, like the soldiers who guard the Tomb of the Unknown Soldier, you will fulfill your duty whether in rain, sleet, heat, or snow, and even take on the forces of hell itself if necessary.

Privates in the U.S. Army who honor their place and do their job honorably and excellently get promoted to corporals and then sergeants, and from sergeants to lieutenants, and eventually all the way up to Generals. It is the same in the Kingdom of God. Not everyone is destined to become a General in God's Army, but promotion is available at every level.

And so is demotion.

People who do not esteem the roles entrusted to them and cast them aside when it pleases them get demoted. Believe me, I've seen it! Well-meaning people who do not understand this principle are meandering about in their spiritual lives not fulfilling their calling because they did not serve honorably in the positions previously entrusted to them. They went AWOL (Absent Without Leave). Therefore, they will receive only partial rewards, if rewarded at all.

The opposite is also true. People who *have* served honorably in the roles entrusted to them and who have persevered are bearing much fruit and are continuing to progress in the Kingdom and will therefore be handsomely rewarded.

The Path of Most Resistance

You've heard of taking the path of least resistance. This is how most people lead their lives. Award-winning Christian rock band of the 1980s and 1990s, *DeGarmo and Key*, promoted a different approach, however, when they wrote and recorded a song on their final album called Carry the Cross, which features the line, "Take the path of *most* resistance." That's the first time I had ever heard it put that way, but it succinctly sums up life in Christ. It is often the path of most resistance. Don't let this discourage you, however, because it has been aptly said that we need not fear resistance, because, after all, a kite rises *against* the wind, not with it. God has in mind for you to rise on the wind!

Have you ever been at a fork in the road, evaluated the two paths before you and decided on purpose to take the path of *most* resistance? This is what some people I have known over the years have done. Some people I have known have stood at a fork in the road regarding what direction to take in preparation for the unfolding of God's call on their lives. In some cases, one path looked like the fast track, and the other was obviously the slower and more difficult path.

One young man I met a few years ago was looking for a church home and received an invitation from a local church in his town to interview for the associate pastor position, complete with a salary package. Because of his connections he felt confident the job was his. His other option, however, was to attend a different church out of town he felt drawn to and come under the wing of that pastor as an apprentice of sorts, with no position and no salary. He was tempted to pursue the instant salary and high-level position close to home. Because he knew enough about God's methodology, however, he ultimately decided to take the road less traveled – the slow, difficult, and hidden path.

People who take the road less traveled will at times be tempted to wonder why in the world they took that path instead of the other. Even so, if they stay on course, then they will reap a reward that will make all the sacrifices they have made pale in comparison. They have chosen the path of wisdom instead of the path of comfort and ease, and at the end of that path lies great reward and fruitfulness.

The Pit of Self-Pity

One landmine to look out for which has blown up many people, derailed them off their calling and prevented them from receiving their full reward is self-pity. Self-pity is a pit of quicksand that can engulf you before you know it. Whether the situation is a delayed fulfillment of one's calling, a less-than-desirable situation in family, job or ministry, or the emotions from having been treated differently than what you expected, self-pity has no place in the life of a person on a mission.

Jesus showed us the proper way to treat the temptation of self-pity. When the Master was explaining to His disciples that He was headed to Jerusalem where He would be betrayed and crucified, Peter spoke up and rebuked the Savior! He said, "Never Lord! This shall never happen to you!" Essentially Peter was trying to get Jesus to abandon His mission and think only of Himself. Peter was tempting Jesus with self-preservation and self-pity. If you know the story, you remember how Jesus responded. It was as harsh a rebuke as the Master ever smacked down on anyone. Jesus had no tolerance for self-pity. He looked straight in Peter's face and addressed him as Satan, because it was Satan's voice Peter had given place to. ***"Get behind me, Satan! You are a hindrance to me. For you are not setting your mind on the things of God, but on the things of man."*** (See Matthew 16:21-23.)

If you have a call on your life, you are going to be tempted with self-pity on many occasions. Take it from me. You must resist this if you want to fulfill your destiny and

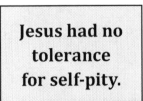

Jesus had no tolerance for self-pity.

receive your full reward. Your calling will likely require you to die to yourself often; it will lead you along a path that seems dark and lonely at times, like the valley of the shadow of death.

The path to your ultimate destiny is much like the path Dorothy and her companions took when following the yellow brick road to the land of Oz and the palace of the wizard. They encountered hindrances, obstacles, disappointments, and delays. And so will you. You can sit down and cry yourself into oblivion like the Tin Man started to do, and if you let that happen you will sit there on the side of the road and rust out while your destiny lays before you the whole time, beckoning for you to get up and get going. You need friends like the Tin Man had; friends who will not allow you to sit there and wallow in defeat and self-pity and abandon the path you are on. You need friends who will look you in the eye and tell you the hard truth about yourself even when you don't want to hear it. If you only surround yourself with "yes men" who just tell you what you want to hear and pat you on the hand when you are feeling low, then you will likely never enter your Promised Land. People who essentially say, "There, there, sweet thing; it's going to be okay; let's go have some cookies and milk and you'll feel better in the morning," are not your friends. People who give you the thumbs up to do whatever your little heart desires and offer you only comfort when what you really need is a kick in the pants are only helping you to hang yourself.

I have to give mention here to a few people in my life who have told me what I needed to hear when I was about to drive my calling over the edge of a cliff. First and foremost, my wife, Donna, as sweet and gentle as she is, has been a lioness when it comes to the call on our lives. She has been the steadying force of our family. She has a soft outer exterior in the way she handles herself, but her inner self is all muscle! When I have bemoaned our situation in ministry and threatened to quit, she simply would not let me! Ministry has been as difficult for her as it has me, but she has been steadier than I have been. If it wasn't for her, I wouldn't still be a pastor. She has not coddled me during my battles with hopelessness. She has told me what I *needed* to hear, not what I wanted to hear. I have almost gotten angry at her for not being more understanding and sympathetic with my plight, but she knows what God has said, and all of my cry-babying won't change her mind. So if she has to have enough faith for the both of us, that's what she'll do. I know one of the reasons God gave Donna to me as my wife was to keep me on track. God knew I would be unsteady and unsure of myself at times, and

He gave me her because He knew she wouldn't play "poor baby" with me but would instead encourage me to keep going until we see the fulfillment of God's plan for our lives and ministry.

There are others who have treated me similarly. I have friends who have had to remind me of God's call on my life and have encouraged me to not let circumstances or other people's actions derail it. On one occasion in particular, they have had to talk me down from jumping off the edge of a tall building, so to speak, with respect to the ministry. I'm thankful for their honesty, because it has saved me from doing something I know I would have later regretted. One of those friends has tracked me down by phone to talk some sense to me before I did something stupid. Of course, during those times I am tempted to rationalize my feelings by telling myself that these lay people have no idea what I go through as a pastor, and they would never go through it themselves if the tables were turned, so who are they to tell me to keep going! But after the emotional dust clears, I always acknowledge the truth of what they are saying and I am thankful they are not "yes men," but God's messengers sent to help keep me on the path.

Listen closely to this advice if you want to receive your full reward: Whatever your calling is, the path – the Yellow Brick Road, if you will – to get there is lined with gargoyles and imps bent on derailing you from ever getting to the palace of the Wizard of Oz. There are wicked witches and warlocks who will resist you and attempt to cast spells upon your mind and turn your thinking into a befuddled bed of goo where you don't know which way is up. You'll find yourself in situations where you think you are still going in the direction of the will of God but instead you are actually doing the will of His enemy, and you will need someone to slap you upside the head, figuratively, and snap you out of it.

It is in the most turbulent of times and/or in times of transition when your spiritual equilibrium is its most vulnerable. It's like piloting a single-engine airplane in dark and stormy weather. When a small airplane is being pounded by strong wind currents and tossed about like a rag doll in a washing machine and it's too dark to see the ground, a pilot's equilibrium can be completely altered. On many occasions where pilots have found themselves in that kind of situation, the confused person behind the controls is forced to face the reality that his senses no longer match what he sees on the instrument panel before him.

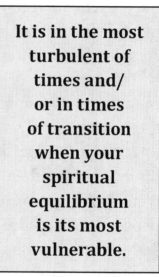

It is in the most turbulent of times and/or in times of transition when your spiritual equilibrium is its most vulnerable.

I heard a story about a pilot in just such a storm whose plane eventually turned upside down, but because his equilibrium was so distorted because of the thrashing about of the plane, he thought he was right side up. Even the control tower kept telling him he was upside down, but he trusted his senses instead. He trusted what he *felt* rather than what he was trained to trust, which was his instruments and the instruction of the tower. When he told the tower he was going to pull up and climb out of the weather, what he actually did was plunge the inverted craft into a dive and crashed to his death.

This parallels the lives of many Christians, especially those in ministry. When times get turbulent, many trust their emotions rather than what they know to be right, and they plunge headfirst into the ground, completely derailing a call of God and sometimes even their marriages. Yes, it feels right at the moment, but they find out only after it's too late the magnitude of their mistake.

It reminds me of a pastor I know who became discouraged and embittered when he lost two-thirds of his congregation. His church was running about 300 people in attendance, and it dwindled down to less than 100. Rather than hanging in there and rebuilding, he closed the doors. The emotional fallout was devastating for him and his family. They have never fully recovered. The pastor trusted his emotions rather than his instrument panel, and he paid a heavy toll.

What I'm about to say next has destiny-altering implications, so remember this and remember it well if you want to walk in God's best.

You can bail out on what God is trying to do in your life and have only the memories of the pain you *partially* endured, *with nothing or little to show for all the time you already invested! Those who quit only have the testimony of quitters. Only those who persevere a long time through trial and don't quit*

have the testimony of a winner. Only those who have overcome something difficult can rightfully be called overcomers!

You can choose to trust God and wait it out patiently for the fulfillment of His plan to unfold in *His* time, serving with excellence and perseverance wherever God has you planted now, and eventually reap a *full* reward that will last for eternity. Too many people, especially in the charismatic world, are looking for God to zap them into their breakthrough or magically refine their character without any painful refining process. Folks, for every one time God zaps someone out of bad character or into a breakthrough of some sort, there are 100 others who God shapes as a potter carefully shapes clay: *through time and pressure.* There's no way around it. This is the way it works. A muscle can't grow without resistance. Neither can a Christian.

Remember, the book of First Peter says sometimes our faith is "tested by fire." The results of a faith tested and purified in this way is glory and honor.

> *"...the proof of your faith, being more precious than gold which is perishable, even though tested by fire, may be found to result in praise and glory and honor at the revelation of Jesus Christ..."*
> **-1 Peter 1:7** (NAS)

It's yours to decide. Do you want to do things *your* way, or God's way?

9

It's Still Your Choice

Let's briefly turn our attention to the Old Testament prophet, Samuel.

Throughout most of Samuel's life there was no king in Israel; God was their only King, and Samuel was the prophet who guided the people with God's words and revelations. The Israelites had different ideas, however. They wanted to be like the surrounding nations and clamored for a king. This upset and troubled Samuel greatly. God then said to Samuel,

> *7"Go ahead and do what they're asking. They are not rejecting you. They've rejected Me as their King. 8From the day I brought them out of Egypt until this very day they've been behaving like this, leaving Me for other gods. And now they're doing it to you. 9So let them have their own way. But warn them of what they're in for."*
> **-1 Samuel 8:7-9** (MSG)

Whoa, whoa, wait a minute! The people didn't reject God, did they? They just wanted a king. They still wanted to serve Jehovah, but they didn't want only a prophet as their authority. They therefore rejected Samuel's leadership. What they did to God's priest, however, they did to God. Again, God's words:

"They are not rejecting you; they are rejecting Me."

God took what they did to Samuel very personally. Even so, although the demand of the people was outside of God's will, He gave them what they wanted even though He knew it was going to cost them greatly. And cost them it did!

Sometimes people operate outside of the perfect will of God even when they believe they are acting in accordance with it. What they are really doing is simply allowing themselves to be dominated by their senses and selfish desires but package it in a way that appears spiritual, thus satisfying their consciences, at least on a surface level. God gives them that right and allows them to go on their misguided courses, and then they pay a price later on.

I know many people, for example, who are both knowledgeable in the Word and tremendously talented but have never learned to put down roots anywhere and submit to God's refining process, making a career of church hopping instead. They lend their talents to churches for a time only to jump ship abruptly and move on to another church after a couple of years or so, starting the process all over again, claiming God was leading them, of course. Some have burned bridges with so many churches that they end up not attending church at all eventually, and instead of using their talents for Kingdom purposes they end up using them for less noble pursuits. Well-meaning and sincere though they might be in some cases, they never learn to submit to God's chastening and discipline, and therefore the call on their lives flounder and fall silent.

I know one man who is a very talented musician and also quite knowledgeable in the Word. However, he has never been willing to submit himself to any sort of spiritual leadership. He has alienated many people in numerous churches, and for a time attended a church where he refused to use his talents to help the struggling worship team. Eventually he stopped going to church altogether and now uses his talents playing guitar in a classic rock cover band. There is a call on his life, but he has never stepped into the fullness of it because he would not humble himself and serve in an area he considered "below" him for any length of time.

It's very sad how people forfeit what God has called them to through unfaithfulness. God gives them that choice. He gives you and I the same choice, and He accepts whatever choice we make, even if the choice will cause us harm eventually. Similar to the ancient Israelites when they clamored for a king and God gave them what they wanted even though He knew it was going to cost them dearly, you and I stand at a similar crossroads. We can do things our own way and reject the temporary discomfort associated with the refining process, claiming it is God's leading, but eventually pay a high price in the end. Or we can submit to God's chastening process and delay our gratification, receiving a reward after we have been found faithful.

Here's a vitally important key concept:

The very definition of faithfulness is sticking to something when your mind and flesh are screaming to do something else.

Faithfulness by nature means looking past temporary discomfort for the sake of future reward. Jesus did this when He scorned the shame of the cross (temporary discomfort) for the sake of the joy set before Him (future reward). [See Hebrews 12:1-2]

It was Jesus, in fact, who taught the parable of the talents, demonstrating the rewards of faithfulness with another person's interests and property and the consequences of unfaithfulness. Jesus also once said,

> **Faithfulness by nature means looking past temporary discomfort for the sake of future reward.**

> ¹⁰*"One who is faithful in a very little is also faithful in much...* ¹²*And if you have not been faithful in that which is another's, who will give you that which is your own?*
> **-Luke 16:10,12** (ESV)

You have to show faithfulness and good stewardship with another person's business or ministry before God will entrust you with more.

To reiterate what God said to me, **what we do to God's church, we do to God.** We can either do things right with the benefit of God's church and His leaders in mind, and, in turn, reap the rewards of doing things honorably, or we can think only of ourselves, our families, and our ministries, and then later reap the consequences of things done dishonorably. It's our choice. We have free will. God allows us to choose. But blessings or curses hang in the balance. As God has said,

> *This day I [God] call the heavens and the earth as witnesses against you that I have set before you life and death, blessings and curses. Now choose life, so that you and your children may live and that you may love the Lord your God, listen to His voice, and hold fast to Him.*
> **–Deuteronomy 30:19** (NIV)

It's as though God was giving the ancient Israelites the answer to the test in advance. It's almost as if He was saying, "Ok, look, I'm giving you a choice here: blessings or curses. I'll lay it out for you. Blessings are good, and curses are bad. Therefore, let Me tell you what to choose. Choose the blessings! Choose life! Choose My way!"

And that's what He is saying to you and me today. Choose His way! Choose life! Choose blessings! It might not be easy in the beginning, but it will be worth it in the end.

Please understand that obeying God or pursuing your calling in the church always involves taking the road less traveled. It means enduring opposition from the enemy, battling your own self-doubts, and, like Moses, Paul, Joseph, and David, may involve long periods of boredom and/or isolation as you wait for your ultimate calling to unfold.

Think about this for a moment. These great patriarchs of the faith were shelved for long periods of time with seemingly no fruitfulness and no productivity for the Kingdom... seemingly. Yet what they didn't see, and what you and I often don't see, is the work going on in the invisible realm, the work of preparation that great future productivity and fruitfulness require.

When I was a worship leader, for example, I sometimes asked myself what I was really accomplishing in terms of Kingdom impact. I had a sense God was calling me to more, and so it made me think little of where I was at the time. Of course, the role of worship leader is extremely important to the Body of Christ because people need to be led in that way. Thus, my doubts about the importance of that role were misplaced from the start. Additionally, I was not taking into consideration the training that position provided for me and the preparation for what God would eventually call me to. If I had not been a worship ministry director, I would not have had the tools to become a pastor. It was a very important season of groundwork preparation for me I was not appreciating or even able to recognize at the time since I didn't know I would eventually pastor my own church someday.

Therefore, resist the temptation to do as the Israelites did in the time of Samuel. Don't clamor to have things your own way when it appears God has you in a season of preparation. Instead, do as many of the patriarchs of old did and submit to the process and watch God unfold your calling in time. The unfolding of one's calling almost always involves seeing it slowly come to pass over the distance of years, *even when you do things right and wait patiently.* If you don't wait patiently, however, and if you take matters into your own hands and try to speed up the process, as Abraham and Sarah did, you will most likely make a mess and slow down or even halt the process.

What so many of God's people do not understand about the unfolding of their calling is there is a honeymoon stage at first as God gives you a glimpse of what He has

> **Please understand that obeying God or pursuing your calling in the church always involves taking the road less traveled. It means enduring opposition from the enemy, battling your own self-doubts, and may involve long periods of boredom and/or isolation as you wait for your ultimate calling to unfold.**

called you to. Can you imagine the honeymoon stage the Apostle Paul must have had when Jesus appeared to him and called him into ministry? He was later also called up to the third heaven and showed revelations he wasn't even permitted to talk about. (See 2 Corinthians 12:1-4.) Now *that's* being called into ministry!

Then the reality of what Paul had been called to set in.

He waited and waited for that ministry to be launched, but he would not set out on his own without the approval of the other apostles. Fourteen years passed from the time of the Damascus Road experience when Jesus appeared to him until the time he actually began to operate in the *fullness* of what he had been called to. If Paul would have acted too soon, he may have spoiled the whole thing, or at least severely delayed the process. But he was willing to wait on God and wait on his spiritual leaders. The rest is history.

When God Seems Silent

Perhaps you, too, find yourself in the same position as Paul. Maybe you feel you have been called of God, and that is likely true. Perhaps, like Paul, you are chomping at the bit but find yourself in a situation where you are not being used like you think you should be, and you are getting impatient. Or perhaps you find yourself doing something you don't really have a passion for but it's where God has you right now. I have some advice for you from years of experience along these lines that will help you, and it's this:

If God isn't speaking, He is speaking!

What I mean is, if you don't have a clear word from God and the circumstances already in place to move you into what you believe God is saying, then God's silence is still something that should be considered a form of communication from on high. Said another way, if God has placed you in a useful role for His Kingdom and He hasn't clearly and obviously said something different, then *His silence is saying He hasn't changed His mind.* Don't move! Don't pseudo-spiritualize a rationalization of doing your own thing by interpreting your discomfort as God speaking.

I had a honeymoon stage when I first stepped into ministry, both as a worship leader and then later as a pastor. In both instances, things were great at first, but then things got hard – *really* hard! There have been so many times as a pastor I have wanted nothing more than to close the doors and just take care of myself for a change. The pressure has been crushing at times. I have struggled with fatigue, depression, broken-heartedness, extreme self-doubts, and the disappointment of the ministry not unfolding in the way and the timing I had hoped. There have been many times I have attempted to spiritualize bailing out on what I know God has called me to, attempting to interpret my discomfort as a sign I'm supposed to be doing something else. But I have learned if God isn't speaking, He is speaking!

Another related lesson I have learned is while God is indeed interested in blessing His sons and daughters in due time, our wise and good Father is not nearly as interested in the temporary comfort of His children as He is our long-term character development and the fulfillment of our callings. He may allow you to stay in a very uncomfortable situation for a lot longer than you want. If you stay the course, however, our faithful God will absolutely see to it you are rewarded for your faithfulness. Just ask Moses, Joseph, David, and Paul. Just ask Jesus! Their lives preach a thousand sermons about the rewards of faithfulness in times when God seems silent. Your life, too, will preach a thousand sermons about the rewards of faithfulness if you stay the course. God's plans for you are always good!

> *"For I know the plans I have for you,"*
> *declares the Lord. "Plans to prosper you*
> *and not harm you. Plans to give you hope*
> *and a future."*
> **-Jeremiah 29:11** (NIV)

As painful as the process of staying the course in spite of seemingly insurmountable obstacles has been at times for Donna and me, one thing I know it has done is provide object lessons to people who have watched us. Yes, we have waivered. Yes, we have made mistakes. Yet, when we get knocked down, we have always pulled ourselves back up again. I have found Proverbs 24:16 to be very true.

Though a righteous man falls seven times, he will rise again.

Someone made a remark to me recently which helped me see what my faithfulness in ministry has done. He said, "I don't know how you do what you do. You're my hero."

He was referring to watching me try to balance the demands of career, family, and ministry for the past several years, absorbing blow after blow relationally, and keep going anyway even when it wasn't fun and it appeared as though my nose was being pressed against the grinding wheel. I didn't realize people were watching that process and taking notes. God has used the process I've been through as a living demonstration of what perseverance looks like. God has used this broken vessel as a living sermon. Thank God for His grace. Like Abraham of old who waivered in his walk of faith, I have not always stood strong. The tempest has battered me at times, and I have been what the Bible calls a "bent and broken reed." I have certainly not seen myself as someone to emulate when it comes to strength of character in this regard. However, the very fact I have been battered like I have but found strength and grace in God to come back time after time has been a testimony to God's faithfulness.

You, too, may feel like a bent and broken reed, battered by the storm. Friend, you can and you must find grace and strength in God. When you are weak, God the Father has a better opportunity to show Himself strong on your behalf, and then you can say like the Apostle Paul, "when I am weak, then I am strong" (see 2 Corinthians 12:10).

If you feel like you are up against the grindstone right now, just remember this:

Life is a like a grindstone; whether it polishes you up or grinds you down depends on what you're made of.

Your destiny still awaits you. Let it unfold in God's time. Walk by faith and not by sight. Choose to stay and fight. In the end, you will be happy you did. I guarantee it!

10

Conclusion:
The Evidence Demands a Response

In 1972, author, speaker, and Christian evangelist, Josh McDowell, gained wide fame for his highly acclaimed book *Evidence that Demands a Verdict*, which details in almost textbook style the evidence supporting the veracity of the Bible and the claims of Jesus Christ as the Son of God. There is much said in the title of McDowell's best-selling book, as it perfectly describes what a mountain of evidence demands, which is a verdict or a response. The gospel of Jesus Christ isn't simply a nice story or even a theological exercise. It is an invitation to mankind by God Himself, and that invitation demands a response.

In this book we have reviewed the Biblical case for serving with honor. Now that the evidence is in, this evidence, too, demands your response.

I suppose a person who has read this book could say I am being self-serving in making the case presented here. Yes, I do have some degree of concern for the church I pastor, of course. That's a legitimate motive. As a shepherd, however, I also desire to see God's people blessed and help them to fulfill the call on their lives. Far too many of God's people experience neither blessing nor fulfillment of their calling because of their lack of stability and commitment. Therefore, in an effort to help people recognize some of the elements which have sabotaged their success and their calling, I have presented my case with a thorough, balanced, and fair analysis of the Scriptures, and I hope you were able to "hear" my heart.

To be doubly sure I have interpreted the Scriptures correctly and am applying them appropriately, I presented the first manuscript of this book to my friend and mentor, Dr. Jerry King, who is a Bible scholar, an apostle to several pastors, and a former pastor himself. He has been in ministry for over 50 years and is the most learned man in the Scriptures I know. If there is any hole to be found in my presentation, he would know better than perhaps anyone. He said in response to the reading, "This is an intelligent, kindly argued, and Biblically-accurate presentation. I cannot find any holes in it."

If what I have presented here is truly Biblical (and it is), then I believe it is not out of bounds to ask everyone manning important ministry positions to respond with a commitment. Whether you are part of our church at Blessed Life Fellowship or you are reading this as a member of another church, a positive response to any

Biblical truth requires a commitment to carry out the mandate of the Lord and His Word.

I realize there are sometimes legitimate reasons to leave a church, but again, God will never lead you out of the church where He planted you simply because of frustration, turmoil, or offense, and especially not if the church lacks a very capable person to fill your spot excellently.

Therefore, there is a decree on the last page of this chapter I encourage you to review and perhaps use to settle in your heart the level of your commitment in doing your job at your church as unto the Lord, which means caring about how you do it, whether you leave it, and if so, how, and when. It is justifiable and appropriate for your pastor to expect everyone filling important ministry roles to be on the same page and establish a firm commitment to stay the course even when times are tough.

Some pastors even require those in their service teams to sign a written agreement form. I'm not going to go that far, however, only because I know even signed agreements are only as good as the paper they are printed on if the person who signed it has not firmly established in his or her heart their level of commitment. I have found that people throw away church memberships and signed agreements as readily as they do used tissues. Those memberships and agreements mean nothing when people get it in their heads they are leaving. Unlike earlier times, a man's word these days means very little, it seems. People have said to me, "Pastor, God has spoken to me, and I know for certain this is the church God has called me to and you are the man I'm supposed to be under," and then they are nowhere to found just a few weeks later. If God's clear call on a person's life is so lightly esteemed, then a signed piece of paper will be esteemed even less.

The declaration at the end of this book, therefore, requires no signature and is not legally binding by the laws of the land. It is included simply to help you understand the importance of the role you play in the body of Christ if you are in ministry, and to take your role and your commitment to it very seriously as if you are serving Christ, not man, because that's exactly what you are doing when you serve the Bride of Christ.

God Allows Restarts

As a last point of consideration, I would like to encourage those of you who have bailed out on God's call on your lives and/or who have left previous churches without being called out by God and done damage in doing so. Be aware that God allows restarts, and perhaps it's not too late for you to go back and make things right and hold up the hands of the man of God if there is still opportunity for you to do so.

In a previous chapter I mentioned John Mark, a young man who abandoned Paul during a missionary journey and afterward changed his mind and wanted to rejoin Paul in a later journey. Although Paul no longer trusted John Mark, the young man obviously learned from his mistake as evidenced by his subsequent faithful service to Barnabas. John Mark did the right thing by going back to Paul asking for a second chance. There were consequences to his previous actions, however, by losing the trust of Paul for a time, but he was able to restore his reputation through faithful service to another minister.

And God gives you the same opportunity.

You may need to go back to the people you abandoned or hurt and ask for a second chance. And if that opportunity is no longer available for whatever reason, or if you have now been connected to another ministry for a significant length of time and cannot leave there without doing similar damage, then you may need to at least go back to your former pastor and humble yourself, apologize and clear the air. God is a God of great mercy, and He can and will give you another chance at your previous place of worship or somewhere else. He allows restarts! Praise God!

This wonderful truth of God's mercy doesn't mean there won't be collateral damage to your previous poor decisions. However, the truth of Romans 8:28 is still true, and God can use your worst decision toward future benefit if you continue to seek Him and endeavor to serve Him honorably going forward.

> *And we know that God causes everything to work together for the good of those who love God and are called according to His purpose for them.*
> **-Romans 8:28** (NLT)

I would like to close by saying THANK YOU to everyone who serves at Blessed Life Fellowship and for the excellence in which you do it. I truly appreciate each of you, and I thank God for your friendship and your partnership in the ministry. May nothing and no one disrupt the work God is doing among us. I truly love you in the Lord. May God bless you!

I also thank those of you reading this who are part of someone else's ministry because you, too, are helping to build up the Body of Christ. If God has called you there, don't give up! Don't misinterpret discomforts or apparent delays as a reason to leave. Be faithful, and God will bless you. There are rewards both in this life and the one to come for pursuing faithfulness and godliness.

> *To the faithful, You show yourself faithful...*
> **-2 Samuel 22:26** (NIV)

> *Godliness has value for all things, holding promise for both the present life and the life to come.*
> **-1 Timothy 4:8** (NIV)

Remember, you have a destiny to fulfill. While that destiny may not necessarily be one of fame and prominence, it is nevertheless extremely important; otherwise, you would have never been born! Large or small, God has a role for you to fill, a mission for you to accomplish, and a Kingdom purpose for you to perform. It's not about you, but about His Kingdom! Though the focus is not yourself, God nevertheless promises reward for those who perform their roles with honor. So do as Jesus did and set your face like a flint toward your destiny, put your hand to the plow and don't look back! I know you will make it!

With the principles discussed in this book now in hand, you are equipped to hear the most precious words you will ever hear on the Great Day when you enter your heavenly reward:

> *"Well done, good and faithful servant!*
> *You have been faithful with a few things;*
> *I will put you in charge of many things.*
> *Come and share your master's happiness!"*
> **-Matthew 25:23** (NIV)

Declaration of Commitment

I, (your name) _____, have been called of God to (name of your church)_____, and I commit to using my calling, my talents, and my abilities to serve His interests here.

If I ever feel led of God to move on from this body, I commit here and now with God Himself as my witness that I will take as a sign of confirmation that there is at least one other sufficiently trained person of equal skill and talent to fill my spot. In this way, I commit to caring for God's church, and not leaving it in a damaged and vulnerable position in my going. I commit to seeing to the needs of God's church in whatever way I can, in good times and in bad, in times of abundance or times of need.

I commit to serving in a way that serves the interests of God's Kingdom, putting the needs of His church as at least equal to my own needs and desires when necessary.

If I ever have concerns or objections, I will not harbor them, but I commit to bringing them to the attention of my pastor or those over me in a spirit of goodwill, openness, and mutual concern for the welfare of God's people and the fruitfulness of His Church.

I make this commitment in the spirit of Psalm 15:

"LORD, who may dwell in Your sacred tent? Who may live on Your holy mountain? The one whose walk is blameless, who does what is righteous...who does no wrong to a neighbor... who keeps an oath even when it hurts, and does not change their mind." **-Psalm 15:1-4** (NIV)

Summary Points

1. God takes it very personally when people take actions that damage His church, even when people make moves that they feel are justified.

2. God does not damage one of His churches for the sake of another by moving people out and leaving gaping holes in the process. When God moves a person, He always provides their replacement.

3. If you feel God is moving you out of one church and into another, but your departure would currently leave a gaping hole in the church where you are currently planted, then a waiting period for God to set all things in order and have your replacement trained and ready to go should be adhered to. It is God's timing, not ours.

4. We reap back in time the damage we do to God's church. When we run out on people who depend on us, similar things may happen to us in time.

5. It is never a good idea to make major moves or decisions during a time of stress, fatigue, depression, transition, or anger. These things impair our judgment.

6. Philippians 2:4 – *"Look not just to your own interests, but also to the interests of OTHERS."*

7. Today's me-culture has very little tolerance for discomfort. But God often uses uncomfortable circumstances to help us develop patience and faithfulness. God does often test His children and refine them through the heat of trials (James 2:1-4).

8. God values loyalty, and He honors it. We should, too. The honorable people in the Bible were those who stuck to their commitments and to the people God had connected them to, even though staying was often not desirable. However, some of the least honorable people, like Lot, paid a major price for thinking only of themselves and not "dancing with the one who brung ya." As Proverbs 27:18 says, *The one who guards a fig tree will eat its fruit, and whoever protects their master will be honored.*

9. The very definition of faithfulness is sticking to something when your mind and flesh are screaming to do something else. Faithfulness by nature means looking past temporary discomfort for the sake of future reward, as Jesus did when for the joy set before Him (future reward) He scorned the shame of the cross.

10. You can bail out on what God is trying to do in your life and have only the memories of the pain you partially endured, with nothing or little to show for all the time you already invested! Those who

quit only have the testimony of quitters. But only those who persevere a long time through trial and don't quit have the testimony of a winner. Only those who have overcome something difficult can rightfully be called overcomers!

Suggested Reading

Planted: Finding Your Place in the Church Today, by Robert Gay
Secrets of the Vine, by Bruce Wilkinson
Honor's Reward, by John Bevere
Undercover, by John Bevere
The Bait of Satan, by John Bevere

Printed in the United States
by Baker & Taylor Publisher Services